THE DAY **METALLICA** CAME TO **CHURCH**

SEARCHING FOR THE EVERYWHERE GOD IN EVERYTHING

JOHN VAN SLOTEN

SQUARE INCH

The Day Metallica Came to Church: Searching for the Everywhere God in Everything. © 2010 by Square Inch, an imprint of Faith Alive Christian Resources, 2850 Kalamazoo Ave. SE, Grand Rapids, MI 49560. All rights reserved. With the exception of brief excerpts for review purposes, no part of this book may be reproduced in any manner whatsoever without written permission from the publisher. Printed in the United States of America.

We welcome your comments. Call us at 1-800-333-8300, or e-mail us at editors@faithaliveresources.org.

Library of Congress Cataloging-in-Publication Data
Van Sloten, John.
    The day Metallica came to church : searching for the everywhere
    God in everything / John Van Sloten.
       p. cm.
    ISBN 978-1-59255-495-9
    1. Presence of God. 2. Spiritual life—Christianity. I. Title.
    BT180.P6V36 2010
    277.3'083—dc22

                           2010001986

10 9 8 7 6 5 4 3 2 1

CONTENTS

PREFACE

Over the past several years I've preached sermons on the movies *Crash, Lars and the Real Girl, Gran Torino, Million Dollar Baby, The Matrix, The Da Vinci Code, The Dark Knight, The X-Files, X-Men, Superman, Spiderman,* and *Cinderella Man*, to name a few. I've drawn on the spirituality of Van Gogh, Rembrandt, and Chagall, on the joy of drinking, the fear of public speaking, and the theology of the oil industry. I've explored the worlds of high fashion and travel, the World of Warcraft, and the World Cup. I've preached on violinist Joshua Bell, cyclist Lance Armstrong, physicist Albert Einstein, and classicists like Bach, Handel, Stravinsky, and Mendelssohn. Recent sermons have looked at photography, oceanography, biology, ecology, technology, and psychology. With the children in our church we've watched *Ratatouille, Finding Nemo, The Incredibles, The Ugly Duckling,* and *Pinocchio,* and we've read *Horton Hears a Who, Green Eggs and Ham,* and *Are You My Mother?*

We've spent our Sunday mornings discussing the human body, our senses, the imagination, and our creative capacities. We've looked at a Redwood tree and a honey bee, at tattoos and at scars. We've studied disabilities and addictions, architecture and cities, politics and business. I've preached on Texas Hold 'Em, the West Coast Trail, gourmet food, Starbucks, the Olympics, and a major league pitcher's fastball.

And, of course, we've listened to the lives and songs of many musical artists, including Coldplay, Green Day, Alicia Keys, Amy Winehouse, Eric Clapton, Bob Dylan, Ray Charles, Johnny Cash, Billie Holiday, Freddie Mercury, Lenny Kravitz, U2, Evanescence, Neil Young, Leslie Feist, Regina Spektor, and Metallica.

It's not what you think (some kind of spiritual gimmick, bait and switch, or shameless church marketing strategy).

It's not that at all.

The reason I preached on all of these topics is because I believe they belong to God. And when things belong to God, they matter and they have something to say.

This book tells the story of a world full of things and people with something to say.

It's about a God who is speaking everywhere.

ACKNOWLEDGMENTS

There are so many people on either side of the decision to write a book.

On the front end, a wonderfully patient and encouraging wife along with beautiful children who've always said it straight; a loving and supportive extended family; a church congregation filled with discerning, creative, and caring co-explorers; and many wise friends and mentors.

On the tail end, a publisher that dared to take a risk on a new author and push the boundaries, shrewd editors who always kept the bar high, and several friends and family members who spent a lot of time reading through some pretty rough early drafts.

At times people's voices have felt synonymous with God's Spirit. For that I'm very thankful.

1 THE DAY METALLICA CAME TO CHURCH

"Look out my window and see it's gone wrong
Court is in session and I slam my gavel down
I'm judge and I'm jury and I'm executioner too. . . ."[1]

—"Dirty Window," *St. Anger,* Metallica, 2003

"But God was very angry. . . ."

—Numbers 22:22

had an uneasy feeling when the call came that Saturday night.

"Hi . . . ahhhh . . . is this Pastor John Van Slo . . . ten of New Hope Church?" It was a woman's voice. She sounded hesitant and a little bit uncomfortable, like she'd never made this kind of call before.

"Yeah," I replied warily. I was in the middle of watching a hockey game, trying to relax before Sunday morning's sermon. I didn't much feel like doing any church business.

"What can I do for you?"

Her next line stopped me dead. Now she was all business.

"My name is Lisa from Warner Music Canada, and I represent the heavy metal group Metallica. Is it true that you're going to be preaching on the band tomorrow morning?"

Suddenly it felt as though I was watching this conversation unfold in slow motion, as if my mind was outside my body. Represent Metallica? What? Really? Then my heart started to race. She went on, "And are you actually planning on using some of their music in your church service?"

I didn't know how to reply. This must be some kind of joke call from someone at my church. OK, it's not really a church in the usual sense—it meets in a community center gym where there's bingo on Saturday nights. We meet there because we want to get past some traditional church barriers—like imposing buildings.

A few friends knew how stressed I was about the risk of preaching a sermon on Metallica. It's such a crazy topic. For weeks I'd been doing all kinds of heresy self-checks. Doesn't Metallica play for the "other team"? Could this get me into a lot of hot water with the church? Perhaps I should have picked a safer musical genre. Or maybe just stuck to the Bible.

For a second I wondered if my prankster friend Geoff was setting me up—he'd probably gotten his wife to call.

"Who are you again?"

Now the voice was more forceful. "I represent Metallica and the band has asked if we could come to your church tomorrow with a camera crew. We'd like to tape the event."

"Are you *serious*? A *camera* crew? Is this for *real*?" The phone started to slip out of my hand as I began to sweat.

"We'd just like your permission."

"Oh no," I thought. "Metallica is going to sue us! Weren't they the band that took down Napster, the pioneer online file-sharing website, when they first started illegally distributing Metallica's tunes? And now they're coming after me!" My heart was pounding in my right temple by this point, and in an apprehensive voice I asked, "What for? Why in the world would Metallica want to get a video of one of our church services? What are they going to do, sue us?"

She must have pulled the phone away from her ear and wondered what kind of idiot she was dealing with. "No. They don't want to sue you. Lars [Ulrich—the band's drummer] heard about your church service this week, and all they want is to see it for themselves. The band left town this morning, and they're already setting up for their next concert, so they obviously can't be there personally."

Dazed, but a little more convinced, I told her that she had my permission. "C'mon down. Bring cameras. Bring anyone you want."

I put the phone down and breathed hard.

For a long time.

Then I laughed to myself.

Did that just happen? Is Metallica really coming to our church? How cool is this?

Sure enough, the next day three sharp twenty-somethings—the Warner Music reps—all dressed as though they were going to grandma's for brunch after the service, showed up at our church, camera in tow. I was wearing my standard preaching attire: khaki knee-length shorts and a T-shirt. Our community was in its typical last minute pre-service preparation mode: some were grabbing bagels and coffee at the back table, others were sound-checking the media and queuing Metallica music videos, and the rest of us were wandering to our chairs as the house band up front opened with four screeching back-to-back, full-on, headbanging Metallica tunes (complete with dry ice and concert lighting).

Strange, perhaps, but that's what we do here.

Then I got up to talk. And something happened. I wasn't thinking about the camera, the crowd, the Warner reps, or the pressure. At that moment I suddenly felt deeply moved, profoundly and reverentially aware. After our band's lead guitarist struck his last chord, the room was vibrating. And as I stepped into the energy-saturated holy silence, I wondered if I'd be able to live up to the power and truth that this music invoked. Would I faithfully honor it and give it its due? Had I *read* it right? The moment actually felt quite strange; as though I could have just as easily been onstage at a Metallica concert, passionately voicing a few existential questions to a heavy metal congregation.

"Do you guys have any idea what's going on here?"

"Do you understand why this music is so deeply relevant to you?"

"Do you have any idea why it matters so much?"

But I wasn't at a concert; I was in church. And I wasn't some kind of rock promoter—I was a preacher. This morning was not really about Metallica; it was about God.

And I felt as though God was there in that moment, bringing truth to it.

I felt that I had a glimpse of what was going on inside the head of the average metal-loving Metallica fan and of what was playing out in a much larger context. Yes, we were all moved by the music, but there was also something bigger than the music at play; there was a Spirit behind the heavy metal spirit.

As I began to preach, it felt as though I were an actor in a play I hadn't written, about to expose the audience to the fact that there was a script, and that we were all part of a plot, and that the Playwright himself was in the room. It raised the hairs on the back of my neck.

———

The gym was packed that Sunday morning. I'd guess that close to two hundred folks who appeared to be non-churchgoing Metallica fans visited our church that day. Many came in response to the free promotion the service got from a local rock station. On the Friday and Saturday leading up to Sunday's service, Calgary's CJAY rock radio ran regular advertisements inviting people to come to church. No joking. CJAY, every hour or so, was announcing (and I paraphrase):

> This weekend New Hope Church, right here in Calgary, is going to be preaching a message on the band Metallica. This news story has gone around

the world. So if you're not doing anything this Sunday morning, then you've got to get yourself out to church!

I was stunned when I heard that announcement in the "upcoming concerts" segment of CJAY's rock report the Friday afternoon before the service.

A friend later told me how Metallica heard about our church service. Earlier that week I had called the *Calgary Sun* to see if they were interested in doing a story on what we were preaching. They were, and they ended up writing a short article describing the event. That article was then read by a DJ at CJAY named Reaper. Reaper, while doing an interview with Metallica's Lars Ulrich after a Thursday night concert here in Calgary, slid the *Sun* piece under the musician's nose.

> *Church to Hear Heavy Message: Sermon on Metallica* . . . unconventional pastor bangs home the message of anger and forgiveness. . . . [Metallica's] a lot like the Old Testament prophets . . . [reflecting] the heart of God against the injustices and the brokenness and the hurt. . . .[2]

After reading the article, Lars exclaimed, "That is *so* cool."

When I heard his response, I couldn't help but smile. Since when has a Christian church received that kind of reaction from a heavy metal rocker? Over the past two decades, this band has received more than its fair share of condemnation from the Christian church. Rarely, if ever, does anyone draw a positive faith connection to their lyrics. Who could imagine Metallica's angry cries resonating with God's?

Maybe God could.

————

This whole Metallica story had gotten its serendipitous start several months earlier. I had just finished preaching a sermon on U2 when a young teenage boy came up to me. Knowing that I'd previously preached on several different musical genres (Evanescence, Lenny Kravitz, Johnny Cash, Igor Stravinsky, J. S. Bach), he wondered whether I'd be open to talking about his favorite band.

"Sure," I said, without really thinking. "What kind of music are you into?"

"Heavy metal," he said.

"Oh," I responded.

We both looked at the floor for a few seconds.

"I'm really into Metallica," he said with a smile.

"Metallica!" I thought. "Never in a thousand years. I hate heavy metal, and I'm 99 percent positive there's nothing spiritually redeemable in their lyrics."

Knowing I had to deal with the boy honestly—I am a pastor after all—I told him I'd pray about it. (This is how many of us give our parishioners the brush-off: defer to

God!) Only problem was, I *did* think and pray about it that night.

The next day, a church novice, someone who couldn't possibly have known any better, called me at home. "Hey John. How are you doing? Listen, I've got two tickets for the Metallica concert this Thursday night [yeah, the band came to Calgary twice that year] and I was wondering if you and Fran would like to go? They're floor tickets so you'll have to stand, but you'll be right up on the edge of the stage."

I laughed out loud and accepted his offer, wondering if this was some kind of divine conspiracy.

Three days later, after digging up one of my old black eighties concert T-shirts, I headed off for some serious metal with my thirty-nine-year-old headbanging wife. (I brought ear plugs.) Palpable energy filled the swelling crowd as we entered the stadium. The place came alive when the opening band, Godsmack, did their set; and it exploded when Metallica took the stage. For two hours they engulfed the huge stadium in a screaming, high-decibel, musical explosion on a rotating platform no more than ten feet from where my wife Fran and I were standing. (It's OK, you can picture me yelling, "Lars! Lars!") At one point, Lars threw a drumstick to the girl on my left. I thought about tackling her for it.

The young couple on my right was equally awestruck. They knew the words to every single tune, and their devotion was total. For two hours they wildly headbanged, risking severe neck injury. But I couldn't help thinking that they were probably more awake and alive in those two hours than I'd been for the past month. At one point a young girl looked at me standing there with my arms crossed and said, "Come on old man, loosen up!"

For the most part the concert was loud and smoky, and the words seemed largely indecipherable to my untrained ears. Eventually I got into it—it reminded me of my youthful partying days—but still, I felt a bit distracted, caught between two poles. On the one hand I wanted to just take the music in (interpret the heavy metal songs via my own personal experience), and on the other hand I wanted to watch others take it in (read Metallica through the eyes and hearts of the other concert participants). I found myself turning around often just to watch those 17,000 souls lose themselves in the experience.

Near the end of the show, as the band was wrapping up with an acoustic ballad entitled "Nothing Else Matters," I sensed a change coming over everyone. Distinctly quieter than the rest of their repertoire, this song seemed to strike a deep chord with Metallica's fans. Boyfriends put their arms around girlfriends. Many sang along with lead singer James Hetfield, and the whole place seemed to be swaying back and forth to the music.

Suddenly the atmosphere became solemn, beautiful.

As I stood there among all those people, I couldn't help but think, "This feels like church." It felt like a community in lament, like a crowd jointly voicing their despairing, disconnected, all-too-human cry to God.

> So close, no matter how far
> Couldn't be much more from the heart
> Forever trusting who we are
> And nothing else matters
>
> Never opened myself this way
> Life is ours, we live it our way
> All these words I don't just say
> And nothing else matters
>
> Trust I seek and I find in you
> Every day for us something new
> Open mind for a different view
> And nothing else matters . . .
>
> Never cared for what they do
> Never cared for what they know
> But I know . . . [3]

At that moment God's love and compassion for all of those angry, despairing, messed-up, beautiful people welled up inside me. I *knew* I had to preach on the message of Metallica. I was sure of it.

But how? Knowing *that* you have to do something is quite different from knowing *how* to do it.

The first thing I did was go online and read the lyrics of every single Metallica song ever written.

Time after time I found myself thinking, "Hey, this sounds familiar . . . and so does this . . . and so does this!" God's truths in the Metallica text were resonating with another set of truths I knew from the biblical story. My lifelong immersion in the Scriptures allowed me to see the God-truth in Metallica's angry songs.

Where exactly did I find that spiritual resonance? Here are a few Metallica/biblical couplets I began to put together:

> Die by my hand
> I creep across the land
> Killing firstborn man[4]
>> —Metallica, "Creeping Death," *Ride the Lighting*

His anger flared, a wild firestorm of havoc, an advance guard of disease-carrying angels to clear the ground, preparing the way before him. He didn't spare those people, he let the plague rage through their lives.
> —God's wrath in Psalm 78:49-50, *The Message*, 3000 B.C.

Justice is lost
Justice is raped
Justice is gone
Pulling your strings
Justice is done
Seeking no truth

Winning is all
Find it so grim, so true, so real[5]

> —Metallica, "And Justice for All," *And Justice for All*

"You wicked people! You twist justice, making it
a bitter pill for the poor and oppressed. You treat
the righteous like dirt."

> —God via the prophet Amos, Amos 5:7, NLT, 750 B.C.

Who are you? Where ya been? Where ya from?
Gossip burning on the tip of your tongue
You lie so much you believe yourself
Judge not lest ye be judged yourself[6]

> —Metallica, "Holier Than Thou," *Metallica*

"You snakes! You brood of vipers! How will you
escape being condemned to hell?"

> —Jesus to the hypocritical Pharisees,
> Matthew 23:33, TNIV, A.D. 30

In song after song, Metallica denounced injustice and
hypocrisy. They exposed and derided the manipulative
milieu of our consumer-driven world. Like Jesus in the
temple, they angrily flipped over the tables of our ever-
consuming and commodifying way of life.

I realized that Metallica was, in many cases, angry about
the same things that angered the Hebrew prophets and
that angered Jesus. They ruthlessly exposed wrongdoing.
They lamented the mess our world was in. They exposed
the meaninglessness of so much of contemporary life.

Given that the prophets were the mouthpieces of God, was Metallica too channeling God's anger?

Were they God's voice?

> Curse the day I was born!
> The day my mother bore me—a curse on it, I
>   say!
> And curse the man who delivered the news to
>   my father:
> "You've got a new baby—a boy baby!" (How
>   happy it made him.)
>
> Let that birth notice be blacked out, deleted from
>   the records,
> And the man who brought it haunted to his
>   death with the bad news he brought.
> He should have killed me before I was born, with
>   that womb as my tomb,
> My mother pregnant for the rest of her life with
>   a baby dead in her womb.
> Why, oh why, did I ever leave that womb?
> Life's been nothing but trouble and tears,
> and what's coming is more of the same.

Are you familiar with those lyrics? No, they're not Metallica's. They come from the messed-up life of an ancient Hebrew headbanger named Jeremiah (Jer. 20:14-18, *The Message*, 600 B.C.); a prophet who despairingly shook his fist at God.

Like Metallica, Jeremiah cried out, "Why? Why such a messed-up world, God? Why was I born into this?" Both Jeremiah and Metallica passionately lamented the fact that things were not the way they were supposed to be.

I continued to study Metallica's lyrics, intrigued by all the biblical parallels, but I had more than just the Bible in mind. Having grown up in the Reformed church tradition meant I also had sixteenth-century theologian John Calvin whispering in my ear. (Doesn't everybody take their heavy metal this way?) In my mind, it was Calvin who first gave me permission to explore the truth found in so-called secular culture. It was his worldview that led me to read the band's lyrics with an ear for God's voice.

"All truth is inspired by the Holy Spirit," Calvin once wrote. All truth—where it really is truth—comes from God, according to John Calvin. Which makes sense when you think about it; where else could truth come from? Who else could be its source? And when Calvin used the word *all*, I think he really meant *all*. All truth—including biblical truth, mathematically formulaic truth, aesthetically beautiful truth, athletically inspired truth, naturally scenic truth, psychologically wise truth, biologically evolving truth, and even righteously-indignant-high-decible-passionately-screaming-for-justice truth. Here I began to find a theological basis for preaching heavy metal.

Calvin again: "Wherever we cast our gaze" we can spot signs of God's glory, disclosed in "the whole workmanship of the universe."[7]

Wherever. For me, that word was obviously big enough to include a band like Metallica.

In an even more compelling passage, Calvin links this openness to truth with the pervasive influence of God's Holy Spirit:

> Whenever we come upon these matters [truth] in secular writers, let that admirable light of truth shining in them teach us that the mind of man, though fallen and perverted from its wholeness, is nevertheless clothed and ornamented with God's excellent gifts. If we regard the Spirit of God as the sole fountain of truth, we shall neither reject the truth itself, nor despise wherever it shall appear, unless we wish to dishonor the Spirit of God. For by holding the gifts of the Spirit in slight esteem, we contemn [show contempt toward] and reproach the Spirit himself.[8]

I took the phrase "secular writers," and replaced it with the phrase "heavy metal music" and then reread the paragraph. And then I felt the heat. Who wants to dishonor the Spirit of God? Or show contempt toward the Spirit himself? By not claiming truth as God's— "wherever it shall appear"—we disrespect God, demean him. We make God into something less than God—a God made in our own image who is way too small.

With this biblical and theological background, I found myself thinking, "Hey, I'm not just *allowed* to look for divine truth in this world, I'm *obliged* to!"

With more than enough material for a good sermon introduction, I then focused my research on the individual lives of the band members. It was here that I encountered some of the personal injustice each had faced. They were angry for good reason, and somehow, by understanding their pain, I found the right heart for more fully understanding their songs.

Lead guitarist Kirk Hammett had an alcoholic, abusive father who regularly beat the living daylights out of him. On his sixteenth birthday Kirk watched his father beat up his mother. As a young boy, lead singer James Hetfield heard his mom say that his dad wouldn't ever be coming back from that business trip. Hetfield also collided with the "Christian" church (sect) that his mom belonged to. After she was diagnosed with cancer, the church told her that in order to be healed she didn't need to seek medical help. She just needed to have enough faith and believe. She ended up dying of cancer.

It's no wonder Hetfield was so angry at the church and at God. No wonder he wrote songs like "The God That Failed" and "Fade to Black." And it's no wonder so much of the band's music speaks of depression, darkness, and despair. These guys knew brokenness firsthand. Reading their personal stories, a deep sense of empathy started growing inside me. By entering into their world, I could understand why they'd be so compelled to vent their anger. It didn't excuse all of their behaviors, but it did help me understand their music on a deeper, more empathic level.

When I read about that spiritually abusive church being complicit in Hetfield's mother's death, I found myself filled with anger. People of faith often draw these lines between the creator God and the world he made, as though the God of the Bible were not also the God of all good science and medicine. This split thinking is also applied to the spheres of secular psychology, business, and entertainment. It leads to the conclusion that there can't be anything good about anyone or anything that's not Christian: Because Metallica isn't a Christian band . . . Because he's not a faith-based counselor . . . Because she's not a Bible-believing businessperson . . . there can't be anything good about them.

What gives us the right to engage God's world this way? How can we treat the elements of God's good creation so callously? God made it all. It's all his. What makes us think we can judge it as harshly as we do? Who says *we* get to draw the lines? No wonder many outside the faith view Christians as naïve and judgmental.

My newly found compassion for the members of the band helped me view them more fairly. And by reading more deeply into their stories I discovered that God was still very much at work in their lives, nudging them, subtly leading them in a healthier direction.

I not only discovered the band members' past hurts, but also their struggle to find new ways to deal with them. James Hetfield, for example, speaks honestly about his battle with anger. He is beginning to recognize that no number of raging songs will make the pain dissipate. Nor would there be enough alcohol to drown it or drugs to deaden it or denial to make it disappear. Hetfield came to a point where he realized that the solution lay beyond these false remedies.

In one particularly revealing interview, Hetfield offers a penetrating look into his own soul. "From the beginning I think people identified with us. Especially angry young men. Learning to embrace that was a big deal, and I've been kind of running away from my life's mission— identifying with people's brokenness and singing about it and bringing it into a stadium and on record—and not knowing it. And I've really tried to put on this shroud of this tough guy who can take it all. And at the end of the day I'm broken inside."[9]

At their second Calgary concert, Hetfield reaffirmed his life's mission. Halfway through their set, standing on one of the upper stages, he said, "How many of you have brought some anger here with you tonight?" The crowd went wild. And then he said, "So have I . . . and I'm leaving it right here tonight." The crowd went wild.

That's how James Hetfield proclaimed his life's mission to 17,000 angry Calgarians.

Years earlier Hetfield (along with Hammett and Ulrich) prophetically wrote a revealing and largely auto-biographical song entitled "The Unforgiven." In it he despairingly explores what a life of "unforgiveness" results in: darkness, anger, and ultimate imprisonment.

> This bitter man he is
> throughout his life the same
> he's battled constantly
> This fight he cannot win
> A tired man they see no longer cares
> The old man then prepares
> to die regretfully
> That old man here is me[10]

In an interview, Hetfield commented on what this song meant to him.

> Yeah, [it was] a showdown with myself. "The Unforgiven" is really blaming other people. I'll never forgive you for what you've done. But at the end of the day it's up to me to forgive, so I can move on and live the life I need to live.[11]

The moment I read that quote I knew I had my sermon conclusion.

A heavy metal star preaching the gospel of forgiveness. I could work with that.

And so I preached God's message through Metallica that Sunday morning, and as a result something changed in our church. Something changed in me.

The story of a church preaching Metallica hit the wire and went around the world. I had interviews with rock stations from all over North America, a five-minute talk on Irish National Radio—even Rollingstone.com carried the story. People could not believe a church would love Metallica in this way.

As I explained my rationale for inviting Metallica to church, all the reporters and DJs I spoke to were genuinely intrigued. I was intrigued. It felt like I was onto something new, on the edge of a new way of living my faith, a new way of doing church. The experience was so alive and so real for our church community it made me wonder . . . If God is this active in the lives of a few heavy metal rockers, where else is he moving? If recognizing God's presence in this one unconventional place has this much power in terms of catching the world's ear, then what would it mean to recognize God in *all* the places his Spirit is at work?

2 WAKE-UP CALL

"Clearly you are a God who works behind the scenes. . . ."

—Isaiah 45:15, *The Message*

"Then the LORD spoke to Job out of the storm."

—Job 38:1

So how exactly does a Christian pastor and his church get to the point where preaching a sermon on Metallica becomes the norm?

It's a long story.

Like James Hetfield's story, it involves both forgiveness and the realization that there may be things going on behind the scenes that we're not aware of.

First, the forgiveness part.

In my message on Metallica I drew a connection between Hetfield's realization of his need to forgive others and the biblical concept of our individual need to be forgiven by God. I said that the best way to fully forgive others is to know and experience the forgiveness of God personally in our own lives. When we know how much we've been forgiven, then we'll have the humility and heart to forgive others.

I'd always known the Christian "math" when it came to matters of salvation. I grew up in a church (not literally, but since I had to go twice every Sunday, it felt like it). But I'd never really experienced the forgiveness equation for myself until I was twenty-nine years old. I was married at the time; we had two children—with one on the way—and I was working as a land developer.

Late one spring evening, I'd just opened my car door in the church parking lot and was about to leave when a pastor friend of mine sidled up next to me and asked, "So how are you doing, John?" Leaning on my Acura's roof, I answered him with surprising honesty.

I had no idea what was coming over me.

I grew up in that church. Sang hymns in its pews. Prayed prayers with the congregation. For the most part thought I understood the whole God thing: be good, attend services, learn your catechism, help out a bit, and, most important, hide your dark side. We all hid our dark sides in that community. No one wanted to be the next scandal, the next failure, the next whisper campaign. We were always so shocked when we'd hear the news. "He's been having an affair with a woman from work. . . . Apparently she's been drinking like that for years. . . . It's all coming out now; they abused their kids."

Strange as it sounds, over the roof of my car I just let it fly—all the junk that had been building up over months, years.

So much of my life had become a lie. I felt like a fake. Everything was so twisted, incongruent, and disintegrated that I didn't know who I was anymore. Out of that confusion the dark truth poked through. It was almost as though I'd reached some kind of guilt and shame threshold, and now everything had to come out. Like the nausea that rises after eating bad food, something inside me was rejecting all of the junk I'd been swallowing.

And now I was exposing my true self to this other person. Initially I was terrified. "How is he going to react to this? Who will he tell?" And yet there was something agonizingly right about what was happening. I had no plan to make this confession. No idea what was really happening. I just started to spew.

Details. I was living a developer's life—in the worst sense of the word. I was a nasty, arrogant deal maker. I would constantly bully and bulldoze architects and consultants. General contractors, normally known for their thick skin and gruff nature, would write letters to my boss complaining about how hard I was on them. My boss would then call me into his office and give me a bonus. Once, I was told, I was so hard on an electrical engineer that he ended up having a mental breakdown. This was what a developer needed to be, I thought. This was who I was. And every Sunday I'd go to church, wearing the same suit I wore to all of those grinding meetings.

I was equally vain and superficial in my personal life. All that ever mattered was how things looked. I defined myself by how people perceived me. It was all a performance. I would say anything to get a laugh, or verbally rip others apart with my caustic tongue if it meant I'd look better.

My mind was constantly engrossed with my net worth. All I ever thought about was the next deal, the next car, the next house, and, sadly, even the next wife. My eyes and heart were always wandering, and I entertained thoughts and visited places that I shouldn't have.

And now my mouth was betraying *me* as this impromptu confession poured out. It was strange and overwhelming. I had no idea what or who was compelling me. Even as I felt shame and guilt at exposing my sins to the light, I also felt surrounded by the freedom and grace of a new reality, by Someone I hadn't previously known was there. That Someone was looking at me, looking straight through me, seeing all of my errant thoughts and actions, fully cognizant of all that had gone wrong, and yet not holding it against me. I felt completely judged and convicted, and at the same time forgiven and freed. It was more real than anything I'd ever experienced before. I began to feel whole again, reintegrated. The love that I felt in that moment was so beautifully merciful, so powerfully gracious, so numinously beyond anything I had ever known.

I cried all the way home. For days and weeks I cried. Confessing to my wife, Fran, I cried. For not being kicked out of the house, I cried. And I could not stop talking about what had happened, about this forgiving God I'd just met. It was all so real and made me feel so alive. I felt like my eyes had been opened for the first time.

Textbook conversion story, right?

Perhaps. Except in my case, I don't recall making what people call a "decision" for Christ. To be honest, I really had no plans to ever tell anyone about that part of my life. That night I was broadsided, mugged by grace.

I've learned since that God can do that. God can do whatever he wants with whomever he wants, whenever he wants, whether the person wants it or not. A divine prerogative, I guess.

During the months that followed my parking lot assault, a lot of things began to change. I often thought about more formally adjusting my life's direction and perhaps changing careers. I kept thinking that I wanted to work for God full time, in some kind of official capacity, like becoming a pastor of a church or something. Strangely, in my mind at the time, it seemed impossible to serve God "full time" as a land developer.

I didn't dare mention these secret thoughts to my wife. As a teen she'd vowed not to marry either a farmer or a preacher. She was just fine with being married to a developer. I built shopping centers. I worked with architects, engineers, and contractors. We lived a comfortable life. To upset all of that would be tumultuous. And my wife had already extended so much grace toward me. How could I ask for more?

As it turned out, I didn't have to. God was not done with his calling process yet. This time both of us were sideswiped.

I was working on an out-of-town project, retrofitting a dilapidated office tower. The goal was to take this tired, outdated structure and make it commercially viable. Early one afternoon, as the project architect was explaining one of his design details to me, I got a call.

"I'm in labor, John. . . . *[heavy breathing]* . . . your mom is going to drive me to the hospital right now. . . . *[more breathing]* . . . you better get on the road quick!"* Five minutes later, I'm whizzing down the 401 and heading back toward Toronto, calmly going over what was about to play out. Baby number three—been there, done that—no need to worry. In a couple of hours I'll be there, and then, a few hours after that, it'll all be over. I wonder if it'll be a boy or a girl. Shouldn't change things all that much at home as we've already got one of each. Hope I get there in time. I'll get there on time. This will not be a problem.

As usual, things were under control.

By the time I arrived at the hospital, Fran was well into labor, and everything seemed to be proceeding normally. Then our obstetrician showed up. As she calmly assessed the situation, her demeanor suddenly changed, "The baby is breech and we need to do an emergency C-section—right now!"

OK, this is different . . . goodbye cozy delivery room equipped with a television and an easy chair; hello sterile operating room . . . hospital greens all around! Fran wasn't all that excited about the change of accommodation, either (something about not wanting to give up the nitrous oxide gas she was so enjoying).

C-sections—they take what little romance there is out of childbirth. Thank goodness for the green sheet that hung between Fran's head and her abdomen. One epidural later, the two of us were having a nice relaxed conversation on one side of the table, while three or four medical staff were frenetically rushing around on the other. We both tried to hide our worry.

Thirty minutes into the procedure, they lifted a baby out of Fran's womb—a boy!

"The cord was wrapped around his neck twice," the doctor said. "Good thing we took this route." I kissed Fran on the forehead and then walked over to the table where they were cleaning Edward up. The nurses all seemed so serious. Must be some kind of C-section protocol, I thought. Staring at my new son, I had this weird feeling. He was kind of funny looking. At first I thought he looked a lot like my brother-in-law's funny-looking kids. I figured he'd grow out of it, and, a few minutes later, I made my "It's a boy" phone calls.

When they whisked Edward off to the "special care nursery, I thought, "Okaaay . . . this is different. No normal family bonding time, but hey, that's probably part of the C-section thing again; obviously they need to put Fran back together first."

As I shuttled back and forth from the nursery to the recovery room, that weird feeling kept nagging at me. I sensed that something was wrong. Edward was getting a whole lot more medical attention than either of our other kids ever had. And he still looked kind of different. I couldn't really put my finger on it, but something was seriously wrong.

I didn't want to voice my concern. I kept thinking that a good father wouldn't have doubts about his son in this way.

Finally I just had to know. So I asked the attending nurse, "Is there anything wrong with him?" She didn't say anything (hospital policy . . . only a doctor can tell the parents). Again I asked her if there was a problem. Silence. Head down, she kept working on Edward. Then—and I still don't know how I knew enough to ask this question—I asked, "Does he have Down syndrome?" The nurse lifted her head and looked me in the eye, tears streaming down her face.

I felt like I'd been punched in the gut.

On that endless walk back to my wife's recovery room, I couldn't even begin to process what was happening. I couldn't see, or hear, or feel anything. I was totally lost. There's no rehearsing for something like this. How could I possibly tell her?

Barely able to enter her room, I just stood in the doorway. When Fran saw my shaken demeanor, her face changed from exhausted to concerned to panicked within seconds. "What's the matter?" she cried out. "What's the matter with Edward?"

She thought he'd died.

When I told her that he had Down syndrome, she exclaimed with relief, "Oh, is that all?"

After making a second set of phone calls to family, and spending the rest of the evening sitting with Fran and the baby, I finally made my way home. Alone in my car I couldn't stop crying. I was not the safest driver on the road that night. When I got home I ran down the hallway, fell face-first onto my bed, and screamed out to God, "I can't do this . . . there is no way in the world I can handle this. . . . I cannot do it!"

"You're right. You can't, John," was the response. "But I can."

No angel at the foot of my bed, no audible words, just that "know that you know that you know" kind of feeling only God can evoke. In the middle of a storm, in response to all of my ranting and raging, there was this mysterious, overriding word of peace, of hope.

But I wasn't able to listen.

Catching my breath, I started to run scenarios of how rotten being the father of a retarded child was going to be (sorry, no political correctness yet). I imagined going to church that Sunday and having to tell the entire community about my disabled boy. How would I be able to talk about him when I wasn't even sure that I could love him?

Then I thought about how crappy things would be when he was eight years old. We'd go bowling with other dads and their retarded kids, and they'd have to put those big bumpers in the gutters because none of the kids would be able to throw a ball straight.

Then I envisioned Edward at age eighteen, sitting at a table in the corner of some high school cafeteria, all by himself, staring at his lunch. Who would ever befriend this severely disabled teenager?

Finally I imagined him at the age of forty, walking down a gloomy corridor of some dismal institution, dirty, disheveled, completely lost, alone, unloved. At that point in his life Fran and I would be dead, and only the state would be left to take care of him.

It was a very rough night.

Three months later, the pain had subsided somewhat and I left home for a weeklong trip to Rochester, New York. A year earlier, I'd committed to taking a group of teens on a community service road trip—six days of helping the down-and-out. I really didn't want to go, but Fran thought it would be good for me.

The first evening we were in town our group attended a special church service designed to welcome and orient us to the upcoming week's activities. At the end of the service, as we all stood to leave, I turned around and looked at the people in the pews behind me. Three rows back, I spotted what looked to be a forty-year-old man with Down syndrome. Beside him stood two very old, frail-looking, gray-haired parents. Sensing I was about to lose control, I quickly headed out to the car and called my wife. I told her what had just happened, "Obviously I'm not ready for this week yet, Fran . . . I think I should come home."

My wife, a very tender and compassionate person, the kind who always listens and understands, knew exactly what to say. "Suck it up, John, right now. There's no way you're coming home, so get over it. Get back into that church right now and do what you went there to do. You've got a group of teens who are counting on you!"

After composing myself, I walked back into the church foyer.

As soon as I walked through the door, the man with Down syndrome saw me. From the other side of the room, he quickly made his way over and introduced himself as Mark. Then he wrapped his arms around my waist, hugged me, and lifted me off the ground. Again the tears flowed. When his parents saw what their son was doing, they were horrified. Rushing over, they told him to put me down. By then I had recovered enough to explain the real reason for my tears. They breathed a sigh of relief and we all talked.

They offered me a different vision of what parenting a boy with disabilities could look like. As the father spoke, I kept looking into his eyes. "He's OK with this," I thought, "with this special needs son he's been dealt. He's at peace with it all. He's OK!"

His peaceful demeanor was at least partially explained by what he told me about the place Mark lived. It was part of a huge state-funded network of assisted living group homes specially designed for people with disabilities. Mark's dad had envisioned the home, started it up, and was running it. Mark was living in one of those homes with a few close friends.

Two days later our group hit the streets of downtown Rochester, and we found ourselves serving lunch to urban homeless people. My job that day was to hand a plate of food to each of the clients. I tried to say something nice or witty to each person to make them smile. Halfway through the lunch rush, I was looking at Crystal's smiling face. She was a drug addict living on the street, about thirty years old, dressed in rags. All her teeth were rotten. As I stared at her, she looked down at her side and introduced the next person in line: "This is my son." An eight-year-old boy with Down syndrome.

It took me a second or two to pull myself together, as I pretended to work in the back corner of the kitchen. Then I walked around to the other side of the serving counter and sat at Crystal's table. Her son's name, coincidentally, was also Mark. We talked for ten or fifteen minutes, about life as a parent of a special needs kid, about Mark's progress and prospects. Crystal didn't seem to grasp how tough her situation really was. Not just living in poverty but having to handle Mark's special needs on top of it all. All she could do was talk about what a good boy he was. The whole time she spoke, Mark kept pulling back his T-shirt sleeve, showing me his biceps and telling me how strong he was.

I kept peering at Mark. He was so beautiful. And he appeared to be quite fit, with hard, well-defined biceps and a lean, taut body. That was comforting for me to see, since, surrounded by early intervention therapists, we'd been working on trying to help Edward lift his head off the carpet because his muscle tone was so poor.

Two days later our community service assignment involved taking a group of disabled teens to the Buffalo Aquarium. Arriving at their group home, I fully anticipated again meeting someone with Down syndrome, and I wasn't disappointed. Sitting on the couch in the living room was an eighteen-year-old named Joe. The moment I sat beside him, he shot me a glare. When I introduced myself and asked him if he'd be joining us for the day trip, he responded by telling me that he wasn't interested at all. It was Friday and he was heading off to a cottage for the weekend with a bunch of his friends. As he spoke he gave off this vibe like, "Why in the world would I ever want to hang around with a bunch of people like you at some aquarium when I could go to the lake with my buddies instead?" You could tell this kid would have friends. He was confident and had a pretty sharp wit. Even though he was a little rude, it was perfect. Like any other teen, he had a healthy amount of disdain for the likes of a patronizing adult like me!

The next day we packed our car and began the long road trip home. Along the way, in one of those totally exhausted, no-one-in-the-car-is-talking moments, I found myself thinking of home. I missed my family, and in particular I desperately wanted to see Edward. Then I realized that this was the first time I'd ever felt that way toward him. I thought, "If I'm missing Edward, that must mean I love him." Three months after his birth I finally realized that I loved my son. At that moment, a deep sense of peace washed over me.

And I began to listen.

The night after arriving home, I sat down to journal about my amazing Rochester adventure. Then it hit me. That night, three months ago, while I was lying in bed running all those awful scenarios of how terrible being Edward's dad was going to be, God already had the events I'd just experienced in mind. God knew. Right down to the last detail, each of my anxious imaginary scenes was recast, retold, and redeemed.

I can still vividly remember the moment: sitting in my living room, laptop on my knees, my whole being trembling with the awe of it all, overwhelmed by the profound reality of divine sovereignty, blown away by the very real and tangible presence of God's providence.

It was like standing before God, seeing omnipresence, feeling all-knowingness, allowing the all-powerful force of my Creator to wash over me. Never before had I experienced or understood what I was experiencing and understanding in that moment.

God loved me so much that he would show me this.

At that precise moment, I knew that something inside me had profoundly and unalterably changed. How could it not? It felt like I'd just been introduced to the Maker of the universe! Like God was walking beside me and then sharply elbowed me into this new direction, onto a different path. And while I wasn't entirely sure what it meant, I felt as though I *did* need to work for him in a more formal sense, full time. I remember saying, "God, if this is who you really are, if you really are this in control, this big, this powerfully and mysteriously at work in the world, then I'll do anything for you, I'll change my whole life. The world needs to know about this!"

This, of course, was God's mysterious plan all along. Within months I began the transition from land developer to church pastor. Not because being a land developer is on God's "B" list, but because God knew that being a pastor was my true calling.

And now, looking back on those traumatic months, I can honestly say that I'm thankful for all that happened. I wouldn't change a thing.

Of course, I still struggle with the pain of parenting a child with disabilities. There are times when I still cry when I think about all the things that Edward will never be able to do. I still worry about his future. And sometimes I wonder about who he'd be without those extra chromosomes. Those questions will never go away. But now, deep down, I sense . . . *I know* that all of this is playing out on purpose, and that I can trust that purpose and know that it's a good one. It sounds strange to say that. But over the years I've had many experiences that have affirmed this truth.

A couple of years back, the most numinous of these experiences played out.

One morning I was praying for my son Edward. It had been fifteen years since the day of his birth, and that morning I prayed a prayer I never could have imagined praying. In all truth and with genuine earnestness, I thanked God for the day of Edward's birth, the actual moment of his entry into our lives. In particular I thanked God for the gift of that day, for how it really was the best thing God could have ever done in our lives.

And then it hit me. How does that happen? How does what was once the worst day of your life become the best day of your life? Same day, same tragic series of events . . . totally different interpretation.

Many times over the course of my life I've experienced this retrospective recalibration of painful events. Time would bring a perspective that sometimes brought about a dramatic redemption of the situation. I wonder if, in the end, we will all experience one big retrospective moment, before the very face of God.

However it works out, I came to realize that it's important to recognize and trust that God is mysteriously at work, even when we cannot see clearly. When we do this—by faith—we're much closer to catching a real-time glimpse of God.

What would it mean to better see God at work in all things right now? Is there a living faith that can give us the eyes to see that even though, on the surface, things look confused, skewed, empty, out of control, lost, or hopeless—like you're caught in a dark and fierce storm—there's this bigger hand, this more powerful wisdom, a mysterious calming voice, still present, still whispering words of comfort?

And so began this extraordinary journey of seeing more and more of God in everything.

3 VAN GOGH'S VISION: TWO BOOKS?

"I must grasp life at its depth."[1]

—Vincent van Gogh

The Church in Auvers, Vincent van Gogh, 1890, oil on canvas

vividly recall my first encounter with a Vincent van Gogh painting.

It was in the Musée d'Orsay on the Left Bank of the Seine, Paris, France. Late spring, 2001. I was on the second floor of this magnificent railway station-cum-Post-Impressionist art museum and had just worked my way though a room full of beautiful Cézannes.

And then I entered that most holy place—Salle 35.

The space had simple white walls and floors with high ceilings and a bright, airy daylight feel; the perfect context for van Gogh's unnaturally natural brilliance. As I turned the corner into the room, the first painting I saw was *The Church in Auvers*; a haunting and prophetic portrayal of the institutional edifice of my faith. My heart leapt. For years I had waited for this moment: reading van Gogh, preaching van Gogh, running my fingers across matte images of van Goghs in so many art books, and now I was here.

I stood for fifteen minutes as though bolted to the floor.

The colors were brighter than I'd imagined; deep cobalt blues and shining citron yellows. All of van Gogh's heavy, signature brush strokes seemed to jump off the canvas. It was everything I'd dreamt it would be, and more.

As I considered van Gogh's work, something mysterious happened. For a second, the painting became a window for me. I imagined Vincent sitting at his easel with this painting before him on a late spring day, 120 years ago, the sun warming his face, a gentle breeze breathing inspiration, his brush moving from palette to canvas and back again. Watching him paint, I wondered what he was feeling about this church institution that had rejected him when he tried to be a pastor years earlier. What was going through his mind as he contemplated the fact that the church had no room for his creatively unique view of God—his vibrant take on the breadth, width, and nature of its Maker? Was he angry . . . distraught . . . or just apathetically resigned? I wanted to ask him, "Where are you at with this whole church thing? Why did you paint it this way?"

"I think I need to touch this painting," I thought.

"I can't do that. I'll set off the alarm."

"But I *have* to!"

Quickly, doing a shoulder check, I did.

Just on the edge, for just a second. I needed to. I wanted to touch the paint that he'd touched. Vincent van Gogh and all that he represented to me was right there on that canvas. Before, behind, and within all those radiant hues was a person. Standing there, I was so entranced by the creative mind of the painter that I just *had* to touch.

Great creators, with their masterful ability to express beauty and power, have an enormous ability to captivate.

Vincent knew this—not about himself but about God. He'd experienced that draw every time he met God in the color yellow,[2] every time he saw Christ in the sun,[3] whenever he'd experienced infinity in the stars[4] or eternity in a peasant's eyes.[5] Vincent never met a sower who didn't preach to him or a cypress that didn't glorify its Maker. Vincent knew that the greatest works of art conceivable—the things that fill this real, material world—were indeed divinely imagined, conceived of, and crafted. Near the end of his short life—two years before he died—he wrote to a friend,

> It is a very good thing that you read the Bible. . . . The Bible is Christ, for the Old Testament leads up to this culminating point. . . . Christ alone, of all the philosophers, Magi, etc.—has affirmed, as a principle certainty, eternal life, the infinity of time, the nothingness of death, the necessity and the *raison d'être* of serenity and devotion. He lived serenely, as a greater artist than all other artists, despising marble and clay as well as color, working in living flesh. That is to say, this matchless artist, hardly to be conceived of by the obtuse instrument of our modern, nervous, stupefied brains, made neither statues nor pictures nor books; he loudly proclaimed that he made . . . *living men*, immortals.
>
> . . . Though this great artist—Christ—disdained writing books on ideas (sensations), he surely

disdained the spoken word much less—particularly the parable. (What a sower, what a harvest, what a fig tree!)

. . . These considerations, my dear Bernard, lead us very far, very far afield; they raise us above art itself. They make us see the art of creating life, the art of being immortal and alive at the same time.[6]

———

That experience in Salle 35 kept me wondering what Vincent was trying to say to us.

Van Gogh painted *The Church in Auvers* two months before taking his own life. So whether he was angry or apathetic or despairing, in choosing the subject he did, it was clear that the church still mattered to him.

Kathleen Powers Erickson was one of the first to introduce me to van Gogh's works, words, and spirituality in her book *At Eternity's Gate: The Spiritual Vision of Vincent van Gogh*. Commenting on *The Church in Auvers*, she notes, "the foreground is brightly lit by the sun, but the church neither reflects nor emanates any light of its own."[7]

As I studied this masterpiece further, I quickly noticed that the church is also painted from the back, with blackened windows and no visible door. There's no time shown on its tower clock and the dull grey edifice is painted in shadow with a dominant black and blue sky looming. Most of the sun's yellow light (yellow being van Gogh's symbol for the presence of God) is falling onto the painting's foreground—the natural grassy path that forks its way *around* the church—onto the only person in the painting; a woman preferring to walk in the light.

Van Gogh's brushstrokes and choices of color in this painting clearly were not accidental.

Nor were they in his *Still Life with Open Bible.*

The van Gogh family Bible lies open to Isaiah 53, a prophetic chapter describing a future Messiah who would usher in salvation as a humble, selfless, suffering servant. Next to it lies a worn copy of Emile Zola's *La Joie de Vivre,* a story about Pauline Quenu, a young girl who is willing to lay down her life for the sake of others, even as they wrongfully accuse her.[8] The obvious and compelling connection: both protagonists are incarnating the same selfless truth: that sacrificial love is the ultimate and only means of defeating the world's evil.

With Erickson's help, I came to understand this master-piece more deeply. She sees it as Vincent's attempt to reconcile his traditional Christian faith with his interest in modern literature.[9] By juxtaposing the two books (a contemporary literary work and the Bible), it appears as though Vincent is asking if the truths found in *La Joie de Vivre* might simply be a modern expression of the truths found in the Bible. She defends this idea by identifying

Still Life with Open Bible, Vincent van Gogh, 1885, oil on canvas

how both books preach the same gospel. Same truth, different story.

Though I certainly agree with Erickson's interpretation, I'm also left with questions.

What if this painting suggests an even more profound understanding of how God speaks? Yes, God does speak outside of the Bible, and truth wherever we find it is God's, but what about the possibility of a truth that *transcends* both texts: a truth that might even *need* both Zola and Isaiah in order to be fully articulated and understood?

What if these texts are talking to each other?

And if they are, what if God is saying something through their conversation?

And if that's true, what exactly is God saying?

Was my passion to hear God in art and culture—movies, sports, science—opening the door to an even greater quest?

It's amazing to consider that God is speaking in these ways today, and that his present day revelations have a mysterious connection to the truth of the Bible. But to now consider this even greater possibility—that the wholeness of the truth God is revealing embraces both of these texts—*that* totally shook my world!

My thoughts began to spin. If God speaks through both the Bible and human culture at the same time, how would that work? What would it mean? How would it affect how I seek out, listen to, and experience God?

These are huge questions, and I feel as though I've only just begun to engage them, but so far I've been able to identify two important implications.

The first implication is what I call *co-illumination*. By co-illumination I mean that the truth contained in the Bible brings light and understanding to the truth contained in broader creation and culture, and the converse: that the truth revealed in creation and culture can illumine the truth revealed in the Bible.

The second implication has more to do with the *counterbalance* this kind of worldview brings. When you believe that God reveals himself through two different texts, it's natural to assume that those two texts are interconnected. This interconnection brings a counterbalancing influence to the reading of either text. God's revelation through the Bible tethers, holds in balance, and offers perspective on God's revelation through nature and human culture, and God's revelation through culture has the same effect on the Bible. If you sincerely believe that God speaks through two distinct "books," the Bible and human culture, then this belief keeps you from making more out of either book than you ought to. It holds your understanding of these two revelations in a healthy tension, and prevents falling into unhealthy spiritual extremes.

The Means by Which We Know God

We know him by two means:

First, by the creation, preservation, and government of the universe, since that universe is before our eyes like a beautiful book in which all creatures, great and small, are as letters to make us ponder the invisible things of God: his eternal power and his divinity, as the apostle Paul says in Romans 1:20.

All these things are enough to convict men and to leave them without excuse.

Second, he makes himself known to us more openly by his holy and divine Word, as much as we need in this life, for his glory and for the salvation of his own.

—Article 2, Belgic Confession, 1567

Co-illumination

Experiencing moments of co-illumination has been the most mind-expanding part of this whole journey of discovery for me. It's more than the excitement that comes through the correlating of truths, more than attaining some new information *about* God or experiencing some kind of cognitive "Aha!" Something more significant happens in moments of co-illumination—something that for me is almost mystical.

It's as though God suddenly moves into real time. Instead of just being a thought, or an abstract idea, or a historical verity, God becomes personally and really present. Somehow, through the connection of ancient biblical God-truths to present day God-truths, a door opens and I realize that Someone is there; an eternal, omnipresent, and timeless Someone. And it's as if that Someone is saying, "I'm the God of both these truths . . . of all these truths . . . all at the same time!"

That's what happened when my son was born. It's what happened at that heavy metal concert. *God* was whispering while I was reading that philosophy of travel book, and knowingly humming along with me to that new U2 song. God showed up when I was watching that riveting movie, smiled when I finally began to understand the depth of that scientific concept, and cheered when I felt so alive attending that electrifying sporting event.

What I'd known all of my life *about* God, through the Bible, had now become something I'd experienced *of* God right there, right then. God's present day word woke me up to his ancient word, and biblical truth became very intimate and real. God became real.

Perhaps the best way to explain how co-illumination works for me is to describe how I experienced it on a trip my wife and I recently took to Italy.

It all started months before we even left.

Knowing that I would be preaching a sermon series on "The God of Travel" when I got back, I made sure to pack a few key things. First, I stuffed my mind with as much contemporary thought on the phenomenon of travel as I could absorb. My primary text was Alain de Botton's brilliant book *The Art of Travel*. De Botton's lucid insights into the philosophy and spirituality of our journeys sensitized my heart and eyes to what I was about to experience. Second, I made sure to carry with me a strong sense of expectation—particularly the expectation that God would reveal himself to me on this trip. And third, I tried to map out some of the Bible's journeying themes. De Botton's thoughts on wandering souls, and how we're all trying to find our way home, reminded me of a few of the biblical portrayals of searching, seeking lives.

It didn't take long for my first co-illumining moment to present itself.

Weeks before our departure, I began wondering about the excitement and anticipation I was feeling. What was it that was making me yearn so passionately for this other land? Why do my experiences of new places always feel so heart-thumpingly alive, as if I were made for newness? I began to recall biblical themes that teach about the God who has made us for the *other* and for the *new*. By nature God is, of course, the ultimate Other; God is eternally new every morning. Then I'd recall Scriptures that describe God as the One who is taking us somewhere—to a new, promised land. According to Christian wisdom we're meant for a perfect place—paradise regained—and for a reunion with God. Until we get there, the Bible teaches, we'll feel like wanderers in a foreign land.

And then the thought hit me, "Is this what's going on in me, God? Is this what my wanderlust means? Is this why travel matters so much to me? Does the excitement triggered by the smell of jet fuel ultimately signal a deep need and desire to get to you?" I thought about how anticipation connects to hope, about how both concepts rely on a compelling future that pulls us. God pulls us. God calls us like a beckoning travel poster. As I experienced the anticipation of Italy during those weeks, I came to better understand my eternal hopes and desires. Somewhere deep inside me, hope and anticipation were talking to each other, and Italy was speaking of heaven.

A month later, I'm standing on the Appian Way, those two-thousand-year-old original stones that lined the way to the ancient city of Rome. As I kneel to touch the stones I contemplate the fact that the apostle Paul walked on this exact road and that this way existed when Jesus Christ strolled the earth a mere one thousand miles east of here. Jesus was here when these paving stones were here, and the Spirit of Christ is here as I am here. For a moment it felt as though I'd stepped outside the confines of time, as though I were meeting God in his timelessness. I thought of Ecclesiastes 3:11: "[God] has made everything beautiful in its time. He has also set eternity in the human heart; yet no one can fathom what God has done from beginning to end."

Feelings of finiteness remained throughout the trip. My brief time on this planet seemed short compared to that of the ancient ruins. Strolling through the Colosseum, my hand would constantly reach out and graze the walls, reminding me to keep the end in mind. Time after time, God's gift of the sense of touch spoke to me in this way. It seemed to concretize my perception of reality, to let me know where I was and remind me that what I was seeing was real. I actually had to take off my shoes in the ancient Baths of Caracalla so that I could walk barefoot on the original mosaic floor. As my feet touched those tiny stones I considered all the long-dead feet that had walked there before me.

A few days later, Fran and I found ourselves on the Venetian island of Burano. There another sense came alive. We'd gotten off at the wrong waterbus stop, one at the back end of the island. But our mistake led to a wonderful co-illuminating experience. It was about 1:30 in the afternoon and we hadn't eaten yet. Before us stood a quaint family-run Italian restaurant with a seaside patio. We sat at a small table tucked in the corner with a grapevine trellis shading us from the midday sun. It was perfect.

We ordered the fixed menu that included a squid, shrimp, and scallop appetizer; the best pasta in cream sauce I'd ever eaten, fresh broiled sea bass with vegetables; a luscious salad whose ingredients were grown in the garden just behind us; fizzy water; a half-liter of wonderful house white (*house* means grown next door in Italy); and, of course, bread. Dessert was simple: two cappuccinos with assorted biscotti.

Through the gift of that meal, we were able to taste and see that God is good. We saw God in the gift of a meal but also in our ability to savor it.

Taste and smell, a neurologist once told me, are processed in the same part of the brain that houses memory. That must be one reason why Jesus did what he did at his last supper. On the Mediterranean night before he was betrayed, Jesus shared bread and wine with his disciples. He said, "Take, eat . . ." Perhaps there are times when the best way to know, experience, and remember God is to taste him.

One week (and twenty-eight cappuccinos) later, we were walking the late-night streets of Florence, heading back to our hotel, when a young girl popped out from an adjacent alley and said, "Free concert starting in five minutes." We'd learned to ignore *free* offers by that point and kept walking, but when we heard music coming from the alley we quickly followed the sound. Soon we found ourselves face to face with a sixty-person choir singing a Gregorian chant. They invited their audience to join them in a nearby church, and we did. The music was breathtaking. There's something about the acoustics of big old Florentine cathedrals—first-generation surround-sound.

Once again, the moment became a co-illumining gift; this time an aural one.

It was no surprise that the choir sang several religious songs, but I felt God moving in that place long before his name was ever explicitly spoken. The gifts of voice and melody were preaching before the first lyric was uttered, as were the elements of sound and hearing. When you think about it, the fact that this aural feast could even be perceived at all is itself a miracle. God came up with the idea of sound, made our ears, and gave us the capacity to hear. The nature of our hearing must have something unique to say, then, about who God is and what God is like.

And it does, if you're listening.

Unlike sight, taste, or touch, hearing is multidirectional. We have the ability to hear from all kinds of different angles, and we're able to take in multiple sounds at the same time: choir voices, stringed instruments, and the shuffling feet of the person beside you.

When I consider that God intentionally designed our hearing this way, I think, "Of course!" If God really is everywhere, speaking to us from all angles all the time, then hearing in a multidirectional way makes perfect sense. The unique physiology of my hearing opened my ears to who God is.

My entire journey was filled with these co-illumining experiences. The ancient rocks that made up the Roman ruins were crying out. Palate-pleasing Italian wines possessed sacramental tones. The sounds of Italy—whether in cathedrals, piazzas, or busy Roman streets—were filled with God's voice. And when the Spirit of God connected their utterances to God's biblical utterances—words that were already familiar to me—it happened. Again and again and again it happened. It made me wonder if every single biblical truth had a creational twin, and if God made it this way on purpose.

Those experiences continue to resonate in my memory. Every time I drink an espresso I remember God's good Italian presence. Every time I hear music—every time I *hear*—I hear God. And the more these experiences happen—with *more and more* of the Bible speaking to *more and more* of life as it surrounds me—the more capacity I have to remember, to contemplate, to experience, and to love God.

The journey continues. And as my list of co-illumining, God-revealing, life-changing experiences grows, I realize that this is the way God intended it to be: seeing his glory, hearing his words everywhere in the natural world, through history and human culture, and in all things.

Even as I experience this in moments of powerful discovery, it humbles me to realize that this was Jesus' everyday approach to life.

Jesus commonly used elements of the natural world—birds and flowers, vineyards and seeds—to connect life in this world with the Creator. He also used products of the culture of his day—wine and wedding feasts, shepherding and tax collecting—to reveal the ways of God. But now I realize that his use of these earthly things is more than mere metaphor. It's about the co-illumination of the ordinary and the ineffable. Christ's weavings of word and world left an unforgettable impression on his followers' lives. Not only did they come to see God's material goodness implanted in everything around them, but every time they would take a sip of wine, witness a wedding, or walk a certain road, they were reminded of Jesus' words. They tasted those words, celebrated them, and were warned by them.

Jesus fully understood and lived the connection between all created things and their Maker. His mind flowed naturally from seeing *God-made things* to the *God who made those things*. He connected everything around him to his Father in heaven. He knew that the *very nature* of created things has something to say.

He moved freely from biblical revelation to creational/cultural revelation—and back again.

> "As for me I cannot understand why everybody does not see it and feel it; Nature or God does it for everyone who has eyes and ears and a heart to understand."[10]
>
> —Vincent van Gogh

Counterbalance

Jesus was free to move between the biblical and creation/culture texts, and he did it perfectly. I'm convinced he wants us—and made us—to do the same. But we fall short.

Our tendency is to accentuate one text over the other, to read one and ignore the other, or to try to overly control the interpretation and meaning of either text. When we do this we lose our balance and misappropriate or misread God's bigger message, sometimes leading to tragic consequences.

But when we read the Bible and creation/culture together, there is a corrective influence at play. Each of these texts not only co-illumines the other, but also brings balance to the reading of the other. By holding to the idea of God speaking both in the Bible and in the present day, we're forced into a humbler reading of both texts. The fact that God speaks today keeps us from limiting God to *only* what he spoke in the past in the Bible. And reading God's Word in the Bible keeps us from misinterpreting his words today.

When held in the proper God-authored tension, this two-book idea brings a counterbalance to our reading of both of God's revelations. It keeps us from falling into extremes like nature worship, human-being worship, or Bible worship.

Vincent van Gogh struggled with the last of these extremes as he encountered it in his family. His parents were very strict in their faith, and for the most part had no room for Vincent's crazy ideas about a God who speaks outside of the Bible.

Their world was perfectly circumscribed by the biblical world alone, and they claimed to know how it all worked. At one point Vincent sent a book he was reading to his parents, hoping that they would read it. It's generally thought that the book was Victor Hugo's *Les Misérables*. Van Gogh's mother wrote to Vincent's brother Theo: "He sent us a book by Victor Hugo, but that man takes the side of the criminals and doesn't call bad what really is bad. What would the world look like if one calls the evil good? Even with the best of intentions, that cannot be accepted."[11]

Vincent obviously disagreed. He wrote to his brother: "But Father and Mother are getting old, and they have prejudices and old-fashioned ideas which neither you nor I can share any more. When Father sees me with a French book by Michelet or Victor Hugo, he thinks of thieves and murderers, or of 'immorality'; but it is too ridiculous, and of course, I do not let myself be disturbed by such opinions. So often I have said to Father, 'Then just read it, even a few pages of such a book, and you will be impressed yourself'; but Father obstinately refuses."[12]

What does van Gogh's father's refusal to read the book say about how he viewed culture? About how he viewed God? It seems that his exclusively Bible-centered faith perspective left no room for any other form of divine revelation.

It would be wrong to dismiss van Gogh's father's attitude too quickly. Many Christians today see no connection between so-called "secular" culture and the Creator. They commonly assume that all there is to know about God can fit between the two covers of a single book. But how can that be?

Since when does *one* conversation with another person reveal everything about who that person is—even if that dialogue occurs over a few millennia (as the dialogue between God and humanity does in the Bible)? How can one word of God contain all God is? It can't.

I'm not saying this to dismiss or belittle the Bible. But I don't believe that we can equate the Bible and God. God can't fit into a book. In fact, if everything that God *is* was written down, "even the whole world would not have room for the books that would be written" (John 21:25).

Through the Bible God invites, calls, and draws us toward him. Every page points to God, but all its pages together cannot fully capture or contain him.

The risk in having an *only-the-Bible-can-teach-me-about-who-God-is* worldview is that we can fall into the trap of thinking that we've got God in hand. We figure that once we know the Bible's contents, we know all there is to know about God. Because we can quote sufficient Scripture, or live by enough biblical principles, we fool ourselves into thinking we really know God.

The moment we think we've got God figured out, we're in trouble. God becomes the object (the thing we're studying), and we become the subjects (the studiers). This is a very dangerous position to assume. When we limit God to the Bible we risk turning the Bible into an idol (something we worship instead of God).

I'm sure Vincent's parents were earnest in practicing their faith the way they did. I'm sure they loved God as best they knew how. But I have to think they could only go so far in experiencing God if they weren't fully engaging and reading *all* that God had written.

Van Gogh's parents were right about one thing: *Les Misérables is* a story that speaks of thievery. Its main protagonist, Jean Valjean, did steal a loaf of bread to feed his sister's children. And, later in the story, he did steal two silver goblets from a kindly priest who took him in. But the story doesn't end there.

One of the compelling powerful grace moments I've experienced occurred in the theater while watching the priest's response to Valjean, caught red-handed. It's a good thing the Royal Alexandra in Toronto, where I was watching the musical version of *Les Mis*, was dark that evening, because I was bawling my eyes out when the priest sang his song of forgiveness. Standing there, with his arms held by the police, Valjean hears the good Father sing, "But my friend, you left so early,/ surely something slipped your mind./ You forgot I gave these also./ Would you leave the best behind?"

Then the priest gives Valjean the silver candlesticks that graced his table, and then he addresses the police:

"So Messieurs, you may release him,/ for this man has spoken true./ I commend you for your duty./ May God's blessing go with you."

To Valjean he continues, in a more serious and deliberate tone: "And remember this, my brother,/ see in this some higher plan./ You must use this precious silver/ to become an honest man./ By the witness of the martyrs,/ by the passion and the blood,/ God has raised you out of darkness;/ I have bought your soul for God."[13]

It touched me so deeply because it brought me back to that church parking lot where I first experienced grace through a pastor's nonjudgmental listening. Christ has bought my life back for God and forgiven me for all my sins, just as Valjean experienced that grace and forgiveness through the priest.

This grace message runs throughout the entirety of Victor Hugo's story. And yet van Gogh's parents would have none of it. I can almost hear the desperation in Vincent's plea "Then just read it, even a few pages of such a book, and you will see. . . ."

How might the van Goghs' world have been transformed if they'd been able to view Hugo's book as a contemporary grace story authored by God?

Having this other God-revealing text (the created order and human culture) can bring a wonderfully balancing influence to a life of faith. The mystery of the Spirit's movements throughout all of creation, all of the time, is almost inexplicable and certainly beyond my grasp. I can never fully *get* how God works, or how big he is.

And that's good; that's very good.

This awareness keeps me in a healthy, hands-off, humble tension. I can't swing too far into the perils of bibliolatry because the book of creation/culture won't let me. Nor can I fall into the worship of nature (and other created things) because the Bible very clearly teaches me that God is independent of the creation and tolerates no other gods before him. God, the Creator, stands apart from the creation. The Bible also teaches that God has revealed himself *most clearly* in the person of Jesus Christ. And Christ, this very intimate and personal icon of the creator God, can most clearly be seen in the Bible. The Bible uniquely reveals who Jesus is, what he taught, and what he came to accomplish.

See how it works? The Bible offers a clear, personal presentation of God; it brings God close, gives God a name, and reveals the new life we have in Jesus Christ. Creation and human culture, on the other hand, speak more obliquely about God, often via a different language, and they reveal more of God's breadth, depth, and enormity.

All of God's *omnis*—omnipotence, omniscience, omnipresence—are *described* in the Bible. But in creation they're *observed*, felt, and experienced. In the pages of the Bible, God seems more *immanent*. In creation, he is unquestionably more *transcendent*. To know God in both senses we need both reading glasses and a telescope.

Living in the tension that exists between these two realities keeps us spiritually grounded; it helps us know our place within the mystery that is God. It keeps us humble— hands-off—depending on God for all understanding.

Co-illumination and counterbalance are two life-changing implications of a worldview that holds that God is deeply involved everywhere and in everything he has made. The more I think about that, the more I realize that Vincent was on to something big.

God *has* intentionally given us two books. We *do* need to read them together, which can be a challenge. While we're familiar with the Bible—having a few millennia of interpretive history under our belts—we're a bit unsure when it comes to reading creation. How exactly does God speak through the cosmos? Where do we begin when it comes to reading the created order and the products of human culture?

4 SPORTS, SPIRITUALITY, AND THE *SENSUS DIVINITATIS*

"You've all been to the stadium and seen the athletes race. Everyone runs; one wins. Run to win. All good athletes train hard. They do it for a gold medal that tarnishes and fades. You're after one that's gold eternally."

—The apostle Paul, 1 Corinthians 9:24-26, *The Message*

"You have made us for yourself, and our heart is restless until it rests in you."[1]

—St. Augustine

"We human beings want God even when we think that what we really want is a green valley, or a good time from our past, or a loved one."[2]

—Cornelius Plantinga Jr.

In late spring 2004, the National Hockey League's Calgary Flames—my new home team—were embarking on their most exciting playoff run in decades. We hadn't won the Stanley Cup since 1989, and now we were in the finals. Calgary was going nuts. There were team flags flapping from nearly every car window. Game highlights made front page news every day. Everyone, it seemed, was totally engaged, fully alive, and wide awake. The sports buzz was palpable, unlike any I'd felt before.

Watching it all play out, I couldn't help but ask, "What's going on here, God? Why is this happening? What's causing us to react to a sports team's success in this wild and unabashed way?"

By now I've come to expect this overwhelming sense that God is *saying something* through this sports euphoria phenomenon. I became convinced that a city going through hockey madness points to something important about who we are and about who God is.

What exactly are you saying here, God?

Then one night, watching a pregame show, it came to me. Rinkside, cohosts Ron Maclean and Don Cherry were talking up the impending battle. The stadium was packed, the crowd was buzzing, the volume cranked high. As the two sportscasters shouted their commentary to each other, I recognized the song blaring in the background over the Saddledome's sound system. "Hey, I preached a sermon on that song three months ago!" I thought.

It's all about our human yearning to be awakened to joy, our deep cry to be made real again. It was the perfect soundtrack for the moment.

The instant I heard the song and made that connection, I knew. This whole event—*any* big sporting event in *any* city—is really about finding new life. It's about waking up to what our existence, our city, our humanity can really be.

In the weeks leading up to this epiphany I'd been thinking a lot about the nature of human desires: why God gave them to us and what they're ultimately meant for. I'd just read the quote at the beginning of this chapter in Cornelius Plantinga's *Engaging God's World*: "We human beings want God even when we think that what we really want is a green valley, or a good time from our past, or a loved one."

We human beings want God even when we think we want the Stanley Cup.

Surely what's going on here is simply this: we're searching for God through a hockey playoff run! It all seemed so clear, and it occurred to me that I should let the rest of our city know this gospel truth. So I made a pitch to the editor of our local newspaper, telling him that I had this great *spiritual* explanation for what was going on in our town. A few days later, the following piece appeared on the editorial page of the *Calgary Herald*.[3]

Prior to the puck drop at each of the last three Flames home games, as Don and Ron were doing their pre-game shtick, Saddledome DJs have been faithfully playing an Evanescence song entitled, "Bring Me to Life." Its lyrics could be the mantra for a city that's experiencing what can only be described as a sporting revival.

Wake me up inside/ Wake me up inside/ call my name and save me from the dark/ bid my blood to run/ before I come undone/ save me from the nothing I've become . . ./ breathe into me and make me real/ bring me to life[4]

Our blood is running now and this is real! It's been fifteen long years since Calgary has felt this alive inside. For many long winters we've been yearning for that bygone playoff era to make the scene, for things to be the way they once were, to be "made real" and brought back to life.

And now, it seems, our time has come. Salvation is at hand . . . this is the day when Calgary goes for the glory . . . four more wins . . . if we can just believe.

It's amazing to consider the impact a hockey team can have on a community. It seems sport, in general, has increasingly wielded this kind of influence over our culture in recent decades. Many a sporting scribe has likened this phenomenon to our innately human

Illustration by Tim Rothheisler. Used by permission.

pursuit of spiritual things. Some even surmise that sport has become the new religion.

Think about it. What's the one thing that has received the most focus and devotion in the hearts of Calgarians in recent weeks? God, or Jarome Iginla? Where have the majority of us found our sense of community lately? At a church potluck, or at a jammed pub on a Wednesday night? Where have we gone when we wanted to experience a sense of awe, transcendence, or victory? To a third row pew near the stained glass window, or to a lower bowl seat at an electrifying Game 6, ecstatically screaming with twenty thousand others, the heat wave from the Flames fire pot washing over us, as Conroy roofs yet another one?

The parallels go on. Where do we celebrate the gift of our amazing human bodies or experience the passionate joy of play? Where do we learn how to persevere and work through our losses, or how to finish well? At what venues do we most often express emotions like hope, faith, and worship?

Maybe we're reading a little bit too much into it all . . . or maybe not. While the fact that sport has supplanted church in these many ways is undeniable, perhaps there's another way to understand what's going on.

Theology coach John Calvin once wrote of a spiritual reality called the *sensus divinitatis*; an inner awareness and compulsion toward God, a sacred homing device implanted in the soul of every human being, including Flames fans. This sense of God runs in us like a river, even though we often divert it toward other things.[5]

The thinking is that we want God even when we think we want the acrobatic beauty of a Kiprusoff save, an extraordinary team effort by a bunch of ordinary guys, or the vicarious thrill of hoisting a Stanley Cup trophy. Could it be that our expression of these desires is really just a pointer to our more eternal yearnings, part of an even bigger game that's being played out?

Conceivably, all that's right about this exciting playoff run is indicative of an even greater Rightness we're all meant to know. We're made to experience the elation and deep soul satisfaction of a sixth game victory; made to have heroes who bring us to our feet screaming "Yes!"; made to live with a sense of hope and anticipation about the future, with a passionate *joie de vivre* coursing through our veins; made to live in real community where a honking horn is seen as a sign of camaraderie instead of antagonism, where total strangers exchange high-fives as we all share in

> the pursuit of a common goal; made to fully engage in and enjoy this amazing game of life we're all playing.
>
> And as for that distant memory we so deeply long for, that former time we all want to re-experience, maybe it goes back beyond 1989, back to the very beginning. Maybe we're all just yearning for things to be the way the Maker always meant them to be, life as this amazing game lived out before and with God.

The *Sensus Divinitatis*

I think it's true.

We do want God when we want a Stanley Cup, a World Cup, a Vince Lombardi, or a World Series trophy. The thing inside us that drives us so naturally to grab hold of vicarious salvation, that inspires us to reach for the glory and compels us be a fully alive human community, is a God-given impulse. God really did make us for himself. And to help us find our way, God built into each of us a mechanism, a homing beacon, an internal spiritual magnet of sorts.

Theologian John Calvin's idea of the *sensus divinitatis* (a sense of the divine) helps us understand the mechanism of this deeply ingrained human trait.

According to Calvin, God has implanted an inherent understanding and awareness of himself into every single person, an awareness that is engraved indelibly on our very way of being human, meaning that we cannot open our eyes without being compelled to see him.[6]

It's as if God is covering both ends of the revelatory equation: by speaking everywhere throughout the created order and by planting within our hearts something indelible that both compels and enables us to listen.

So what does this inner sense of God, this sense of divinity, look like? And how exactly does it work?

Like most God things, the *sensus divinitatis* is not easy to define. This spiritual movement resides deep within us, operating quite mysteriously and speaking a language that results in a different kind of knowing. *Sensus divinitatis* knowing occurs behind the more readily apparent evidential kind of knowing.

Philosopher Alvin Plantinga explains it this way:

> It isn't that one beholds the night sky, notes that it is grand, and concludes that there must be such a person as God: an argument like that would be ridiculously weak. It isn't that one notes some feature of the Australian outback—that it is ancient and brooding, for example—and draws the conclusion that God exists. It is rather that, upon the perception of the night sky or the mountain vista or the tiny flower, these beliefs just arise within us. They are *occasioned* by the circumstances; they are not conclusions from them.[7]

Something of God's mystery in and behind the outback connects with something of God's mystery (the *sensus divinitatis*) deep inside of me. God *there* speaks to God *here*, and I am awakened.

Something of God's truth in football, in the *scrambling out of the pocket, launching one downfield, and hitting the receiver in the end zone* quarterback, connects with something of God's *I'm made to make the play* passion in me. And when I recognize that moment as authored by God—working both sides of the equation—I'm doubly alive! And the moment seems perfect, *just right*, the way things were meant to be.

Plantinga calls this "just right" feeling a *doxastic experience,* "the sort of experience one has when entertaining any proposition one believes. Entertaining, for instance, the proposition that $3 + 2 = 5$ or that Mount Everest is higher than Mount Blanc *feels* different from entertaining one you think is clearly false—$3 + 2 = 6$, for example, or *Mount Blanc is higher than Mount Everest*. The first two feel natural, right, acceptable; the second two feel objectionable, wrong, eminently rejectable. As I say, this experience is always connected with operations of the *sensus divinitatis*."[8]

This is the kind of knowing that the *sensus divinitatis* results in: a natural, acceptable sense of rightness. A deep within you, *know that you know* sense of truth, beauty, or meaning. Of course, this sense can be awakened by a miraculous display of nature, but it can also be invoked by the handiwork of human nature: a *just right* forward pass, a haunting aria, or a Nobel-winning theory of social networking.

There is a divine Rightness behind each of these rightnesses that reveals itself all around us and deep within us. God is present and at work on both ends, whether we know it or not.

So when we fall in love with a new Coldplay song or with a venerable Rodin sculpture, when we're deeply moved by a great film, we can thank God for that. God made us to be moved in these ways. God made what's moving us. And once we've tasted God's truth in any of these inspired places—again, knowingly or not—we find ourselves seeking to repeat the experience.

This is where our yearnings and desires come in. We want to experience that rightness like children do, crying, "Again! Again!" God's goodness in the thing we seek and his presence behind it compel us to keep on searching. That search is particular to each human being and yet common to us all. We want to get ourselves back to the garden (of Eden that is) where everything was right and good and whole.

> "Late it was that I loved you, beauty so ancient and so new, late I loved you! And, look, you were within me and I was outside, and there I sought for you and in my ugliness I plunged into the beauties you have made. You were with me, and I was not with you. Those outer beauties kept me far from you, yet if they had not been in you, they would not have existed at all. You called, you cried out, you shattered my deafness: you flashed, you shone, you scattered my blindness: you breathed perfume, and I drew in my breath and I pant for you: I tasted, and I am hungry and thirsty: you touched me, and I burned for your peace."[9]
>
> —St. Augustine

Every search for human meaning and significance and beauty is about getting back there.

Which makes me wonder if the specific nature of our desires deserves a little more attention. If we examine them more closely, perhaps they have something important to teach us about ourselves and about God. But where to start?

Evidence of the *sensus divinitatis* is everywhere: in our human yearnings for love, security, meaning, comfort, beauty, peace, satisfaction, joy, justice, hope, unity, respect, rest, adventure, a sense of belonging, of mattering, of being found, and in our deep and insatiable desire for victory and for glory (especially in a playoff game).

> "You, God, are my God, earnestly I seek you; I thirst for you, my whole being longs for you in a dry and parched land where there is no water."
>
> —The Hebrew poet, Psalm 63:1

> "Sometimes I wish someone out there will find me./ 'Til then I walk alone."
>
> —Billy Joe Armstrong, "Boulevard of Broken Dreams," Green Day

> "Find me somebody to love. . . ."
>
> —Freddie Mercury, "Somebody to Love," Queen

> "Even when men knock on the door of a brothel they're looking for the love of God."
>
> —G. K. Chesterton

Yearnings like these occur everywhere in human experience, and, while skeptics may seek to explain them in other ways—they're the result of a faith gene or some vestigial evolutionary adaptation—I'm convinced they were put there by God to keep us searching for him.

And I believe that each of these deep yearnings—their specific nature and direction—have something to say about what it means to be human; about *how*, *why*, and *to what end* God made us.

How so? First, if God created and implanted these yearnings, then surely *what we yearn for* is, in some way, akin to what God created us for. Our hearts are compelled to pursue things that emanate from God's heart. Second, if God implanted all of these yearnings with the intent that they draw us to him, then surely each and every one of them is meant to find its ultimate fulfillment in God.

The math is simple. We long for security and God wants us to be safe; God *is* security. We seek meaning and purpose and God wants us to have meaning and purpose; God *is* our meaning and purpose. We desire inner peace and God wants to bring peace to the entire cosmos; God *is* peace. We see all of the pain and oppression of this broken world and our hearts break and yearn for justice; God yearns for it too. God is the source and standard for all justice.

In the arena of sports we experience passionate yearnings for victory and endgame glory. To know Christ is to know ultimate victory and an unimaginable moment of glory when God's kingdom will be unveiled at the end of time. The whole message of the Bible, and especially of that last mysterious book called Revelation, is that God wins. And when God wins, humanity wins too.

When I applied this kind of logic to the Calgary Flames' hockey playoff run, it made perfect sense. We really are made for God, and everything we do, even when we do it wrong, is an attempt to find our way back to God. If this is true, then what would it mean to start seeing all of our human yearnings through this interpretive lens?

The more I think this way, the more excited I become about engaging the broader culture with this understanding of human life. It provides a natural setting for God to meet people in the places where they are already most passionately seeking him.

Bad Aim

Still, it's not quite as simple as it might first appear, and this way of thinking requires some care. Sometimes—often, in fact—our yearnings get misdirected or misapplied, and they fall short in our pursuit of God. It's what happens when we fall into idolatry. In his essay "The Weight of Glory," C. S. Lewis wrote:

> The books or the music in which we thought the beauty was located will betray us if we trust to them; it was not *in* them, it only came *through* them.... These things—the beauty, the memory of our own past—are good images of what we really desire; but if they are mistaken for the thing itself they turn into dumb idols, breaking the hearts of their worshipers. For they are not the thing itself; they are only the scent of a flower we have not found, the echo of a tune we have not heard, news from a country we have never yet visited.[10]

I get what C. S. Lewis is saying here because I've fallen into this trap far too many times. I fall in love with the thing I desire instead of the God who's behind it. There is something within me that tricks me and leaves me short. I need to be constantly aware of this.

The same thing happens in our church. I'll hear people's response to an editorial or a sermon, and I'll realize that they're still worshiping the fashion scene, the Calgary Flames, the van Gogh painting, or the film. Right after I've finished making the most compelling case I can make that the desires we express are actually meant to be met in God, and that God is behind the thing being examined, people still walk away thinking, boy, do I love that band, that film, or whatever the object of desire happens to be.

In response I want to say, "Look, there's nothing wrong with loving the band, but there's much more going on—and I don't want you to miss it." It's a bit frustrating but also very enlightening. Our desires are powerful and they are easily deceived. The *sensus divinitatus*, it seems, can lead us in either of two directions: toward the false light of idolatry or toward the true light of God.

But the risk of idolatry must not keep us from exploring God's good gift of the *sensus divinitatis* and the good human yearnings it evokes. We need to be aware of where our desires can go wrong, but then embrace the God-rightness in them as well. This approach opens the door to a whole new view of God's real-time presence and power.

The life we're living is much more than some kind of game. If we had any idea why our yearnings and desires are so powerful, if we grasped their true source and meaning, we would change. Everything would change. We would see the deeper truth of our God-drenched world, and I'm convinced life would be considerably more beautiful.

A recent movement called Improv Everywhere reminds me of how this all works. The mission of this exuberant undercover group is to create "scenes of chaos and joy in public places."[11] Basically they want to wake people up to the meaning of life by messing with the norms, by brightly coloring an ordinary black-and-white life. Watching online videos of their stunts, I can't help but think they're doing the exact same thing we're trying to do as a church: wake people up to the beauty and power of the moment, help them see what's really happening. These folks are hitting the same God-yearning nerves that we are.

One of my favorite improvs is entitled "Best Game Ever." In this stunt organizers send a major league camera crew, some big-time NBC sports announcers, a full-on PA system with jumbotron, and a few rabid fans to a neighborhood Little League game. Even the Goodyear blimp shows up. What a delight to watch the faces of the children and their parents as the experience unfolds!

They're dumbfounded. No one can really believe what's happening. Initially they're not quite sure how to respond, but after a few minutes they decide to go for it and fully live into the extraordinary moment.

As viewers, we vicariously share in the glory of these young kids and their families. It's hard not to tear up when you watch this happening. Your heart swells with delight and joy. And this happens because we're meant for this kind of glory! God made us this way. God made life to be this way.

If we only had eyes to see, I think we'd realize that there's no such thing as a run-of-the-mill kids' baseball game. Every game is filled with this kind of potential. Whenever a group of children and parents get together to play, to compete, to be community, a most extraordinary event is occurring.

We're doing what God made us for. God is there. And in the profound sense of the absolute rightness of it all, God draws us there too.

The World Cup and Heaven

A couple of years after that hockey playoff run, the connection of sports with Calvin's old *sensus divinitatis* roared back into my life. It was 2006, and soccer's World Cup was again in focus.

As the frenzy built around the upcoming matches, I started thinking of devoting a Sunday morning service to God's presence in the World Cup phenomenon. As we began to plan for the service, I discovered that the final game would be played on Sunday, July 9, at noon.

What could be better than a service on the theme of the Cup followed by a World Cup party around the big-screen TV?

As our sermon team got to work, a biblical reference point easily came to the fore:

> Then I looked and heard the voice of many angels, numbering thousands upon thousands, and ten thousand times ten thousand. They encircled the throne and . . . in a loud voice they sang: "Worthy is the Lamb, who was slain, to receive power and wealth and wisdom and strength and honor and glory and praise!" Then I heard every creature in heaven and on earth and under the earth and on the sea, and all that is in them, saying: "To him who sits on the throne and to the Lamb be praise and honor and glory and power, for ever and ever!" (Revelation 5:11-13).

The connection? It seemed to all of us that this global event—around which people from every corner of the world, every tribe and tongue and nation, focused on one game, one ball—provided an experience of what can only be called glory.

It's a foretaste of the final and complete glory that arrives when God brings heaven to earth, of the universal elation and cheers from every corner of the world that echo the loud voices cheering the Lamb (Jesus) who was slain on the throne of heaven.

> "What makes the World Cup most beautiful is the world, all of us together. The joy of being one of the billion or more people watching 32 countries abide by 17 rules fills me with the conviction, perhaps ignorant, but like many ignorant convictions, fiercely held, that soccer can unite us all."[12]
>
> —Sean Wilsey

U2's Bono put it another way in a voiceover for an ESPN commercial:

> It's a simple thing, just a ball and a goal. Once every four years that simple thing drastically changes the world; closes the schools, closes the shops, closes the city, stops a war. A simple ball fuels the passion and pride of nations, gives people everywhere something to hope for, gives countries respect where respect is in short supply, achieves more than the politicians ever could. Once every four years a ball does the impossible; and if history means anything, the world as we know it is about to change.

Hope for change is an irrepressible human desire. We long to live in a world where nations are allowed to be fully and uniquely themselves—nationally, ethnically, religiously, socioeconomically—and yet still sing their anthems side by side in the stadium of life.

We yearn for a world where the playing field is truly level, where a poor boy from Algeria can become a global superstar, where Ghana can defeat the United States.

We crave the kindness and humanity of a Muslim Iranian football squad that brings pre-game flowers to a Catholic Mexican goaltender who just lost his mother.

We're desperate for a force that can cause wars to cease, just as qualifying for the World Cup tournament did for the Ivory Coast.

And deep inside, we want to believe that there really is "one thing" that can unite us all. We hope against hope that there is some greater force for good that can capture our imaginations; that can cause us to take our eyes off our limited, sometimes selfish selves and allow us to see the freedom of an unbounded, bigger picture. We want to be a part of something significant, something larger than life, something beautiful!

In a world rife with sectarian violence, terrorized by elusive evil, plagued by the forces of poverty and illness, strained by anxiety and stress, bogged down by boredom and ennui, deeply searching for a greater meaning—a world that's lost its ability to play—we long for a better reality, a new way of life.

The World Cup ignites our hopes and dreams for this glorious unity of nations. But of course, a game cannot ultimately usher in God's kingdom or save us. World Cup hopes and dreams can only point us to deeper yearnings that only God can satisfy.

5 CRASH: WHEN GOD COLLIDES WITH A MESSED-UP WORLD

"For all have sinned and fall short of the glory of God."

—Romans 3:23

"I just woke up this morning and I thought I'd feel better. You know? But I was still mad . . . and I realized . . . it wasn't about having my car stolen. That's how I wake up every morning. . . . I'm angry all the time. And I don't know why. Carol, I don't know why."[1]

—Jean talking to a friend, Crash

I was standing in front of a classroom full of Christian high school students when the teacher asked her question.

"But what about the problem of tacit approval? Pastor John, aren't you giving your approval to the whole film when you teach about God's truth in parts of a movie like *Crash*?"

I didn't like the question. It presumes that truth can be walled off into sealed compartments: "Watch the right movies, avoid the wrong ones, and you'll be fine." That's just too simplistic. But I got where the teacher was coming from. She was concerned that I was presenting a worldview that would leave her students in a morally tenuous position. By finding anything good in this very dark film with all its sex, violence, profanity, and general depravity, she worried that I would be giving my approval to everything in the movie.

A group of kids at the back of the room suddenly tuned in to the conversation. You could tell by the way they leaned forward to catch my response. It was like they really wanted to see this R-rated film and were hoping for a little spiritual support for their position: "But Mom, there was this pastor in our social studies class today who said that it's fine to watch *Crash*!"

So I took a moment to think about my answer. And then I told her that I thought her logic was faulty. Just because you see *some* good in a movie like this doesn't mean you're claiming it's *all* good. What I was trying to say was, it's not all bad, and we need to consider how to handle that fact.

I have to admit I felt a bit uncertain and confused at that moment. A part of me was drawn to her moralizing worldview. Why get involved with anything that reveals so much human degeneracy? In the church where I grew up, I was taught that it's better to avoid that kind of content. And yet I couldn't agree with the teacher. Even though *Crash* is filled with scenes portraying the shards of human brokenness, it also communicates a vision of wholeness. And that bigger message is so powerful that it overshadows and recasts those lesser concerns. I couldn't ignore the greater truth.

So I paused for another second, and then I said, "I see what you're concerned about. If you open the door to whatever goodness is in *Crash*, you risk exposure to badness. That's unavoidable, I guess. But it's also life. I agree that you have to weigh these things. But I still think it's a risk worth taking . . . for the truth's sake, and for God's sake.

"If this really is the way the world is—everything a confused mix of good and evil—then kids need to learn how to find their way through this stuff; we all do," I said. "And besides, by not naming God's truth in these places, aren't we running the risk of an even bigger omission in another direction? What if our avoidance leaves us in a place where we miss out on all kinds of instances of tacit worship? When I watched *Crash* and experienced the power in its redeeming finale, I found myself in the middle of a huge divine epiphany. Whether the screenwriters and directors knew it or not, in my estimation they were being God's agents."

I wondered whether this phenomenon of tacit worship could also be happening anonymously in all sorts of places. Earlier in that classroom, we'd talked about God's truth in science and music and in us as human beings. What if that atheistic astronomer is really worshiping God as she explores star-birthing galaxies? And what if that agnostic cellist, whether he's conscious of it or not, is actually praising his Maker as his dancing fingers and sweeping bow draw exquisite sounds from his instrument?

On the flight home I thought about the teacher's question and the whole problem of good and evil being mixed together. And then it struck me.

The problem with *Crash* is also a problem with the Bible! When you consider the adult content found in the holy Scriptures—rape, incest, prostitution, racism, adulterous murder, polygamy, genocide, drunkenness, lying, cheating, infanticide, and homosexual gang rape, to name a few—it's clear that the Bible would also get an R rating. A man sleeps with his daughter-in-law, thinking she's a prostitute. A woman drives a wooden tent peg through an army general's head while he's asleep. King David, who's been ordained by God, has a loyal soldier killed in order to cover up an adulterous affair with the soldier's wife.

The Scriptures are filled with all kinds of violent, ignorant, and unholy characters. We find errant prophets speaking God's truth and crooked scoundrels entering into holy covenants. God used unbelieving nations to accomplish his will; he used Egyptian pharaohs, Assyrian and Roman kings, and even ladies of the night (Jesus had a prostitute in his family tree).

Obviously God is willing to work both sides of the street with a less than stellar cast. God has the ability to say what he wants to say, to get done what he wants to get done, regardless of whether or not *we* have our act together. I bank on this fact every Sunday morning—every day, in fact. Regardless of our human frailties, God continues to move and speak. Thank goodness!

God works in and through the messiness, the malignity, the sheer horror of real life in the real world.

My excitement with *Crash* had begun months earlier when a member of my church could hardly wait to tell me about the film: "You have to preach on this movie, Pastor John. It's one of the most powerful film experiences I've ever had."

You've got to love it when church plays out like this.

So I headed out to the local Cineplex and discovered that he was so right. As I watched the film I was hit by several co-illumining moments. The way I see it, *Crash* is really a story about our desperate need for God.

This 2006 Academy Award-winning motion picture approaches that need from two directions. First, it presents a brutally forthright commentary on the human condition, and second, it offers the hope that someone, somewhere, is able to make sense of it all.

"Nobody leaves this movie unscathed," said *Crash* director Paul Haggis. He was right. I felt sideswiped, exposed, as though my own inner thoughts had been turned inside out. I could not enter the world of this film and leave my own culpability behind.

The primary vehicle in *Crash*'s message is racism. But not simple racism—it includes all kinds of human prejudices: a Caucasian gun store owner toward a Persian man and that same Persian man toward a Hispanic locksmith. A corrupt white cop toward a black woman, another black woman toward that same white cop. The rich toward the poor, the poor toward the rich. A man toward a woman, a woman toward a man. A mother toward her son, a son toward his mother. And last, but certainly not least, we, the viewing audience, discover our own hidden prejudices.

In engaging the film we realize we're no different than the story's characters.

We're just as broken, just as guilty as they are.

Crash slaps you in the face with this truth. It strips you down and pulls the rug out from under your self-denial. In a brilliant act of storytelling, the film takes the spotlight of human depravity, the one we so readily aim at others, and jarringly turns it back on us.

In one scene, two clean-cut young black men are walking along, talking about the unfairness of racism and the discrimination of stereotyping. As viewers we find ourselves walking alongside them, nodding in agreement with their assertions, sharing their incredulity at the injustice of it all. Then, in a shocking plot twist, the two pull out concealed weapons and ruthlessly carjack a rich white couple. In that moment, all our broad-minded liberal sensitivities fly out the window.

The same thing happens when a very nice Korean man, an innocent bystander run over by the fleeing carjackers, turns out to be a slave trader. Our stereotypes of relationally broken reality are not as clearly defined as we'd like to think.

Good and evil are not easily discerned. They hang around in each other's shadows. They intermingle and wear each other's clothes. Half the time we can't even tell the difference between the two.

And *Crash* just keeps on unpacking us.

A rich white woman screams her fears to her husband that the heavily tattooed Hispanic locksmith working in the adjacent room is a gang member. With the locksmith, we're sickened as we overhear her racist rant. With the woman, we're sickened as we overhear ourselves.

And in what was for me the most disturbing subplot of all, we meet a savior—a man who appears to be the only admirable character in the film—a white cop named Tommy. We seethe with him at his partner's blatant bigotry. We stand with him when he's challenged on his racial idealism. We celebrate human potential with him when he saves a black man caught in an explosive confrontation with police.

And we die with him when he ends up shooting a young black hitchhiker because of a meaningless prejudicial misunderstanding. We share his shock as he sits in his car. We feel sick about who we really are.

I tell you, at that point in the film I was ready to throw my hands up. I felt such despair for the human condition, now so achingly personal. It reminded me of words from the apostle Paul that seemed to perfectly describe my feelings at that moment:

> There's nobody living right, not even one, no-body who knows the score, nobody alert for God. They've all taken the wrong turn; they've all wandered down blind alleys. No one's living right; I can't find a single one. Their throats are

gaping graves, their tongues slick as mud slides. Every word they speak is tinged with poison. They open their mouths and pollute the air. They race for the honor of sinner-of-the-year, litter the land with heartbreak and ruin, don't know the first thing about living with others. They never give God the time of day.

—Romans 3:10-18, *The Message*

Crash's depiction of the human condition was so real, it made me wonder, "Is this what humanity is really like? Are we this perverted? This twisted? This filled with self-denial? Have we all turned aside and become corrupt? Is there anyone who does good, even one person? Who's going to save us from this mess?"

I felt totally busted. This is who I am. Sure, I'm not acting it out as explicitly as the characters in the film, but there's little difference in my inner thoughts and motives. And I'm like this, the Bible teaches, because of something called sin—a spiritual virus that's corrupted my system like a computer worm taking over a hard drive. Software, hardware, *everything* starts to malfunction. Even worse, my computer gets taken over by the malicious intent of another. And because the problem is system-wide, I can't clean it from within.

How can anyone untangle the mess we're in, let alone hear God's good voice in the midst of it all?

Some would say we can't.

With sin wrecking everything—including you and me—there's no way to ever clearly see your way to God's truth. Some people say the world is just too broken. They say it's naïve to think you can discern God's good voice in the cacophony of human degradation.

But then I think about the biblical story again and those messed-up characters who fill its pages. I remind myself of the God pictured there who is both above and within this mess, mysteriously directing it and still speaking through it.

This gives me hope.

My hope does not rest on the internal resources of any one of the characters portrayed in the Bible (apart from Jesus!). It starts outside of them. In that holy story, God himself crashes into a hopeless situation and remakes it from the outside. And just like in *Crash*, that remaking occurs when humanity seems to be at its worst, when our degradation hits bottom, when we're crucifying God's Son.

While we were busy hammering in the last few nails, acting out our denial-based self-righteousness, God tearfully looked down on us. He looked down at the mess we'd made and the suffering of his Son and screamed out, "Enough!"

And all the while Jesus looks into our eyes and prays, "Father, forgive them."

The moment we were at our God-damning worst, God was at his best.

And what's really captivating is this: the whole time this story is playing out, we have no idea what's going on. It's as if we're being saved behind our backs, from outside the system. While we were still messed up and messing up, Jesus died for us. This idea is central to the Christian gospel.

It's also central to *Crash*, in a subtler yet undeniable way.

As with any good film, the underlying theme is communicated through a few clever visual cues. In *Crash*, every time the camera looks down on the city or on a particular scene from above, it's as if we're offered a "God's-eye" view of things. The director seems to want to tell us that someone is seeing all this from afar. Which makes me wonder if an even greater Director is doing the same thing.

Crash's storyline takes this idea of someone watching and goes further, opening our imaginations to the possibility that this someone is also mysteriously acting through all of the events portrayed in the film; someone is getting things done and moving circumstances along.

A distraught man is saved from himself when the gun he attempts to use for a murder has only blanks in it. A man who's engaged in human trafficking just happens to get hit by an SUV. Two desperate human beings—a nasty police officer and the woman he's recently abused—

surprisingly meet in a most unimaginable way and a dramatic reconciliation occurs.

In the Bible God does the same thing. God isn't a detached, hands-off deity just hoping we poor souls work it all out. God sees. God acts. And like all good screenwriters, God writes his story in a way that accomplishes his directorial purposes.

Consider the details of the reconciliation between that police officer and the woman he's abused. In this scene we have a bigoted white cop who just happens to end up being the first officer at the scene of a terrible car accident. The black woman whose life is hanging in the balance, in an overturned vehicle, is the same woman he'd physically assaulted the night before. Initially both are horrified at the situation. But the car she's stuck in is about to explode.

Then something mysteriously takes over.

A heroic sense of duty rises up within the police officer; he risks his life trying to free the woman from the burning wreck. Having no choice, she lets go of her more-than-justifiable anger and trusts him to save her.

Arm in arm the two run from the fiery scene, falling into a tearful embrace. Then the car explodes and the camera pulls up into the sky.

It's as though some greater force for good is working behind the scenes. God caused circumstances to play out in exactly this way, stepping in and saving them despite themselves.

Hold on. Did I just write God into the script of *Crash*?

Why not? Who else could orchestrate events so perfectly and bring so much good out of such a hopeless situation?

But this is fiction!

It is, but surely the Spirit of God can move wherever it wills, even within the hearts of fictional characters. Surely the Spirit of God can move in the heart of a screenwriter to create a character whose actions would reveal the heart of God.

Why would we think that God couldn't or wouldn't be at work behind the scenes, shaping a story like this? I believe God moves in fictional places all the time—in films, books, and songs—just as he moves in the places we call "real." God's Spirit is at work in every facet of our day-to-day lives, even when we suspend reality to enter into a great Hollywood myth. If that's where we are for a couple of hours on a Friday night, why wouldn't God meet us there? God is the God of all myth and every imaginative moment.

As I sit in a theater experiencing the transforming power of that unimaginable rescue scene in *Crash*, I'm also aware of God's behind-the-scenes operations in my own life and in my world. The film story and my own life story meld together, making me aware of God's reality in every layer of life—the real and the fictional—on the screen and in the texture of my experience.

In this way *Crash* became another means of God's active involvement in my life. And because the film so vibrantly depicts the reality of contemporary life, God could make his point even more powerfully. The director's brilliance in filming this story, in revealing not only the evil that resides in my soul but also the fact that Someone out there is working to fix the problem, made the Bible's teachings more vivid and direct. The movie reminded me of who I am on both fronts. But it didn't *just* remind me.

When God's truth in *Crash* spoke to God's truth in the Bible and in my life at that time, an amazing dialogue ensued. I was brutally confronted by my own depravity and at the same time I was filled with hope for the God who works in and through the messiness of my broken humanity.

Some people were offended when I first drew the parallel between *Crash*'s despicable characters and me. It was as though they thought, "Surely we're not *that* bad." In fact, deep down inside, I am that bad. *Crash* helped me recognize this through characters that had the familiar feel of my own struggles, prejudices, and blind spots.

At the same time, it made me feel hopeful. *Crash* presented a compelling picture of a mysterious force that was making good out of the mess of reality. It opened my eyes to see more vividly what I had been taught in church all my life: God is at work in our world. It set me to wondering how much God still moves behind the scenes in this messed-up world, rewriting reality's ugly script.

A mystical, haunting song called "In the Deep," by Bird York, plays behind *Crash*'s closing scenes. It's yet another layer in which we hear the voice of the Spirit of God through this film.

> Thought you had all the answers to
> Rest your heart upon
> But something happens
> Don't see it coming, now
> You can't stop yourself
>
> Now you're out there swimming
> In the deep
> In the deep
>
> Life keeps tumbling your heart in circles
> Till you let go
> Till you shed your pride, and you climb to heaven
> And you throw yourself off
> Now you're out there spinning
> In the deep
> In the deep[2]

This call to admit that we don't have all the answers, to shed our pride, to "let go," speaks to my heart. Too often

I feel driven to do exactly the opposite, and it never gets me there. Every time I try, I crash.

When I heard this song playing behind *Crash*'s broken and despairing scenes, I wondered if God sings something similar over our lives.

At the end of York's song, there's one final message that's cut from the film's soundtrack but is part of the lyrics on the audio recording. If you listen closely to the recording, it's there right at the end. Just as the closing instrumental segment is finishing up, you hear York whisper, "If you want to be given everything, give everything up."[3]

Hearing her, I heard Jesus whisper, "If you try to hang on to your life, you will lose it. But if you give up your life for my sake, you will save it" (Luke 9:24, NLT). If we want to hear God's voice today, then we need to let go. Let go of the idea that we can control how and where God speaks. Let go of all the things inside us that say that's impossible.

6 *NO COUNTRY FOR OLD MEN:* EVEN THERE?

"If the rule you followed brought you to this, of what use was the rule?"[1]

—Psychopath Anton Chigurh, *No Country for Old Men*

Perhaps the risk of tacit approval isn't as big a concern as I thought. But I still wonder how far to go with all this.

How much darkness do I endure to locate one beacon of light? How much garbage should I dig through to find one pearl of truth? Is there a point where the cost is just too high—a moral or ethical tipping point I'd better not pass? A point of no return? A line that shouldn't be crossed?

These questions continue to dog me on this journey, and I've come to realize that the "line" often moves.

A few years ago, at The King's University College in Edmonton, a student came up to me after a lecture I'd given entitled "Seeing God in Metallica." He was from Africa, and after thanking me for the talk, he said with polite firmness, "I want you to know that I listen to gangsta rap. That's my music. It's the music I grew up with. And you need to realize that all the points you've just made about the legitimacy of God's Spirit being at work in Metallica also apply to this music."

The student made this comment in response to a story I'd just told about a live phone interview I'd had on a Seattle rock radio station months earlier. That interview went something like this: "Hey Pastor John, thanks for joining us this morning. Before we talk, we've prepared a little something special for you to listen to . . . a bit of Metallica metal audio mash-up."

For some reason I felt like ducking, but how do you do that on the radio?

They played their sixty-second audio collage: segments of five Metallica hits interwoven with snippets from raving fundamentalist televangelists. It was intended to slam both me and the church. When it was done, one of the DJs asked, "So, Pastor John, what do you think about that?"

Realizing that they were assuming I had stereotypically trashed the band in my message—what else would a church do?—I said, "Actually, I found it quite humorous. And you should know that we used four out of those five Metallica songs to start our service off that Sunday morning."

Then I clarified a little. We didn't do what they presumed we did with the band. In fact, we did the exact opposite. We talked about where God was working in good ways through Metallica's music.

Those two DJs were totally caught off guard. I imagined them looking at their producer through the studio window with hands raised, shrugging, "What do we do now?" What they did was this. Sensing that I'd turned the table on their table-turning tactic, they tried to turn it back again.

"God in Metallica, eh, Pastor John? So what's next? Are you planning a sermon on gangsta rap for next Sunday?"

I was scrambling a bit at that point. Not entirely up to speed on the nature of the genre (misogyny and a big gun culture were all I could recall), but figuring by the DJ's tone that it was really bad, I said, "No, never . . . I'd never preach that kind of music in church!"

The three of us then nervously laughed. Deeming the interview a draw, the DJs wrapped things up and cut to a commercial.

That is my music. The music I grew up with. . . .

The African student didn't say it directly, but as he applied my "God in Metallica" ideas to his gangsta rap music, he made his point abundantly clear. Don't judge something you know nothing about. You can't possibly understand unless you've lived in my world. After he left the classroom I just sat there shaking my head, asking God, "Even there?"

I can't tell you how many times I've caught myself saying these words, and when I do, I'm usually in a state of surprised shock. But why wouldn't God be there, in seemingly unlikely places?

And so the line just keeps moving for me. If I decide to only go as far as an old-school metal band like Metallica, I meet someone who lives in the gangsta rap world. If I plan on only engaging the "safe" cultural-creational texts, I meet a person who's experiencing God beyond the boundaries.

To be honest, it's hard to know where to stop.

So I look to Christ's example. Surely the Son of God knows where to draw the lines—where to go and where not to go. And then the answer becomes clear: "Don't stop here. . . . Not yet. . . . Go further. . . ."

Jesus went further. Jesus is the embodiment of the God who goes further, entering into our messed-up world as a baby. He went further than I can ever imagine. Heaven's perfection entered into earth's shadows. Now *that's* moving the lines.

Why would he do this? Because there is no piece of this good yet broken world that God does not claim as his own. God loves this world and will travel to the farthest boundaries to reclaim it. Jesus' life reveals God's passion. The gospels speak of how Jesus was criticized for hanging out with the wrong sort of people: prostitutes, lepers, and tax collectors. His behavior drove the "good" religious leaders of his day crazy. It's understandable, really. They were drawing lines, something I was struggling with too. They would never be caught fraternizing with this kind of crowd. In fact, they got so upset they even called Jesus a friend of sinners (they meant that as a bad thing).

If I really am going to follow Jesus' lead, then I need to cross lines like he did. That means approaching the world with the same embracing love I see in Jesus, a love that mirrors the Father's heart. Jesus never lowered his moral standards in order to engage lost souls. In fact, he led with the highest moral and ethical standard—love.

It's not that he somehow lived above the fray, or that he was unerringly nice, but that in the muck of human life he lived in the light of God's love and truth. And in his definition of the word, *love* meant hanging around the raw edges with broken people, shining the light of God into their dark places.

Jesus went that far and still goes that far. So when I consider the kind of Spirit that is now moving in our world, in all those edgy places, in all those truthful ways, I remember that it's Jesus' Spirit—his breath, his heart, his passion, his mission, his love moving across the boundaries to embrace a lost world.

This is the heart of God. So why would I ever be surprised if God shows up in places I don't expect? Perhaps I should change my expectations and open my eyes wide. Of course God is at work where things are at their worst. Of course God's Spirit is active there, preserving, keeping, and re-making his good creation.

Why would a loving God ever leave anyone—any lost soul or faraway person—alone? How could God ever do that with his creation?

Saint Augustine once said that there "cannot be a nature in which there is no good."[2] Augustine cannot be accused of entertaining a low view of God, and his words offer a powerful corrective to how some people tend to view the depraved state of humanity. Yes, sin infects everything, but it does not have the capacity to destroy anything. The

Creator reserves that right. The worst people imaginable still bear the image of their Creator. It's their inherently good gifts that get twisted and perverted for evil.

I've heard echoes of God's voice speaking in the darkest places in literature, media, and the arts; in the rough life and tunes of Amy Winehouse and in the raunchy life story of Queen's Freddie Mercury. Even in places I usually don't feel comfortable going, like the Coen Brothers' film *No Country for Old Men*.

Since I suffer from an overactive imagination, I usually avoid intense thriller/slasher movies. They make me lose sleep. So when someone suggested I watch this bleak and dreadfully violent 2007 Academy Award-winning film, I hesitated.

"You've got to watch this movie, John, it's really dark but it's very powerful," my friend said.

"Why? Is there a redemptive theme there that I could preach on?" I asked.

After a long, recounting pause—you could tell he was replaying the movie in his head—he said, "No, I don't think there's anything redemptive in this story at all. But you should still get out and see it!"

I finally mustered the courage to see it a few months later when the DVD version came out (not quite as scary on the small screen). The film fully lived up to its dark billing. And there, even there, I found God speaking.

This film tells a morbid tale about a psychopath named Anton Chigurh (Javier Bardem). He is embarking on a murderous rampage in an attempt to chase down some stolen drug-deal proceeds. Pursuing him is a nearly retired sheriff named Bell (Tommy Lee Jones). Picture Tommy Lee Jones's face and you'll understand exactly what his character was all about. Bell was a decent officer who started his career in a more decent time. But the world has changed, and now he's struggling with what it has become. Throughout the film, I found myself resonating with Sheriff Bell's increasing disillusionment with trying to police people who don't know right from wrong any more. Every wrinkle on his face seemed etched by his daily struggle with a society that was falling apart around him.

In one conversation with a fellow sheriff, Bell bleakly confesses, "I used to think I could at least in some way put things right. I don't feel that way no more"[3] Later, in a more personal and spiritual conversation with another old acquaintance named Ellis, he admits, "I don't know. I feel overmatched. I always thought when I got older God would sort of come into my life in some way. He didn't."[4]

Bell's world had become unhitched. The bad guys get away with murder, and the good guys end up with nothing. Justice gets mugged, raped; it's a distant memory from a bygone era.

As the film staggers into ever-expanding violence, you begin to wonder if Bell is right about the state of the world. But then two "hopeful" events occur.

Near the end of the film, we see the despicable Chigurh driving away from another murder, the most heinous because his victim seemed the most innocent. As he makes his escape from this sleepy West Texas town, he calmly drives his car down an almost empty street. The camera view then switches and we see the scene play out as though we were the driver. It's a beautiful day and nobody's around. The intersection ahead is clear and the light is green. Chigurh appears to be making another clean getaway, and then *BANG*. He gets T-boned by another vehicle running a red light. The brute force of the collision leaves him badly broken, and he hobbles away from the accident scene into oblivion.

No, he doesn't die in the end. That would be too "Disney" for the Coen brothers. But this jarring reminder that there may be some kind of providential justice out there, that evil does not go unseen or unpunished, was hopeful (at least a little bit hopeful).

This tiny pinprick of hope widens as the film moves to the final scene.

Bell, now retired, is in his kitchen with his wife early one morning. He tells her about a dream he's just had that involved his long-deceased father. The film ends with Bell describing the dream.

It was like we was both back in older times and I was on horseback goin' through the mountains of a night . . . goin' through this pass in the mountains. It was cold and snowin', hard ridin'. Hard country. He rode past me and kept on goin'. Never said nothin' goin' by. He just rode on past and he had his blanket wrapped around him and his head down, and when he rode past I seen he was carryin' fire in a horn the way people used to do and I could see the horn from the light inside of it. About the color of the moon. And in the dream I knew that he was goin' on ahead and that he was fixin' to make a fire somewhere out there in all that dark and all that cold, and I knew that whenever I got there he would be there. Out there up ahead.[5]

And the film ends.

The juxtaposition of these two small incidents—an accident pointing hesitantly toward justice and a promising dream—with the hopeless violence of the rest of the film, reminded me of a biblical psalm, of all things.

There's a moment in Psalm 73 in which the writer, in despair over the way evil people unjustly prosper and the good get trampled, comes to realize that what appears to be an inequitable reality is not the ultimate reality: "[Evil people] clothe themselves with violence. From their callous hearts comes iniquity; the evil conceits of their minds know no limits" (vv. 6-7). He goes on to say, "The wicked get by with everything; they have it made, piling up riches. I've been stupid to play by the rules; what has it gotten me?" (vv. 12-13, *The Message*).

That last line could easily have come from Sheriff Bell himself, and from all of the rest of us who've struggled with the same troubling inequities.

But then the psalm writer has an epiphany.

Halfway through his despairing poetic rant, he sees that reality is not merely as it appears on the surface. Entering into God's space, taking in God's view of things, he sees a greater, more hopeful, and more just reality.

> Until I entered the sanctuary of God.
> Then I saw the whole picture:
> The slippery road you've put them on,
> with a final crash in a ditch of delusions.
> In the blink of an eye, disaster!
> A blind curve in the dark, and—nightmare!
> We wake up and rub our eyes. . . . Nothing.
> There's nothing to them. And there never was.
>
> When I was beleaguered and bitter,
> totally consumed by envy,
> I was totally ignorant, a dumb ox
> in your very presence.
> I'm still in your presence,
> but you've taken my hand.

You wisely and tenderly lead me,
and then you bless me.

You're all I want in heaven!
You're all I want on earth!
When my skin sags and my bones get brittle,
God is rock-firm and faithful.
Look! Those who left you are falling apart!
Deserters, they'll never be heard from again.
But I'm in the very presence of God—
oh, how refreshing it is!
I've made Lord God my home.
God, I'm telling the world what you do!

—Psalm 73:17-28, *The Message*

So even there—in what seems to me one of the darkest of dark Hollywood films—the Spirit of God is whispering, saying something that sounded a lot like something he'd said before.

Through a bleak and bloody motion picture, God's Psalm 73 truth was speaking—whispering its hopeful message. And perhaps there was meaning in the presence of the dark depravity as well.

After all, in Psalm 73 God wasn't just speaking through the good stuff, through those last few glimmers of hope. In a sense God was also saying something in the midst of all that was so terribly messed up. When life goes on as though disconnected from its Maker, as though God is absent, it loses its moral bearings and the wheels fall off.

Sometimes God lets people live with the consequences of that choice, at least to a certain point. Life without God is hell, as both Psalm 73 and *No Country for Old Men* preach in an unsettlingly brutal way. Yes, God says something through the presence of goodness, truth, and justice, but he also says something through their absence. He says, "This is what life is like when you live as though I'm not here."

————

Years ago, when I was just beginning to understand this whole idea of God speaking through culture and creation, I had a hopeful dream. During those months, I had been losing a lot of sleep. Controversy over my preaching was growing and people were leaving the church left, right, and center. Every week, it seemed, I'd get another long e-mail explaining how theologically errant I was. At the time, I felt pretty confused and hard done by. I wondered if I should just give up. And then I had the dream. It was just a dream . . . but it gave me hope.

In my dream I was viewing the earth from way out in space; like you'd see it on Google Earth. As I was looking at the planet, I realized that God was standing there right beside me. As I stood there, God's presence communicated two powerful truths to me, both at the same time. The first was the fact that I was a barely perceptible pinprick on the face of that planet. The humility of that fact was exacerbated by the second truth: a very clear sense that

I was only there for a finger-snap, a mere nanosecond. Again, this was a very humbling thing to recognize.

While I was seeing who I really am, God conveyed who *he* really is: infinite, beyond all knowing, the maker of that tiny planet and of the vast cosmos that surrounds it. The One who is, who always has been, and always will be. God's holy timelessness and spacelessness were so immense, so dwarfing, and so powerful that I woke up saying, "Of course it's true, of course you can, of course you are! This is your world, and you're God, and you have the power to speak by whatever means and wherever you want."

It was a hopeful dream because I felt in my bones that it pointed to the dizzying reality of an infinite and accessible God.

Christians believe that Christ really did make the scene as a human baby, that he did die and descend into hell, and that three days later he was resurrected. We believe that he ascended into heaven, and is now seated at the right hand of God.[6] We believe that all things are now held together "through him and for him" (Colossians 1:16). We believe that the same Jesus, who is above it all, was also there at the beginning, before it all. We believe that he played a part in creating it all—a big part. The Bible clearly teaches that nothing was made apart from him (John 1:1-3). We believe in an eternal Jesus who was there in the beginning and is there at the end; who *is* the beginning and the end (Revelation 22:13). And who right now says that he is making all things new (21:5).

This is what the Bible teaches about who Jesus is now, filling the universe and yet right beside us.

If this is who Christ is, if this is how far he's willing to go, how can I not dare to discern the light of his love in the darkest places?

7 PUSHBACK: IS THIS HERETICAL?

"You should be ashamed of yourself. You are not a man of God. . . ."[1]

—hottamale02

". . . it's wrong to worship anything that is not of the Holy Trinity. Neil Young is not a prophet . . . and it is a sin to say that he is."[2]

—MrSunshine124

". . . don't they know that Dr. Seuss was an atheist?"[3]

—chimmister

It's no fun being perceived as a heretic.

Understandably, the accusation often comes with a level of concern that's in direct proportion to the unconventionality of the message. People get most angry when I talk about things that seem to be, in their minds, antithetical to the nature and mission of God.

Unfortunately, I choose those kinds of topics often, not to stir the pot but because they actually make the larger point most powerfully. If God's goodness and truth are present in a place like this, then God must surely be moving everywhere. Citing God's message through *The Simpsons*, Neil Young, Seven Card Texas Hold 'Em, or the oil industry brings this greater possibility home. And that unsettles people. Saying that God is speaking through these unconventional voices, and then bringing these voices into the church, seems sacrilegious to some. But I think it's the exact opposite. I think that when we recognize a God who chooses to move in these and all kinds of places, God is honored.

Facing Objections

After preaching a sermon on God's voice through Coldplay, this comment was posted to our YouTube video:

> This is the most ridiculous, theologically incorrect message I have ever heard in a Christian church. I would even go so far as to say this is heretical.

God moves in our lives through Scripture or his Holy Spirit. I love Coldplay's music, and there may be some spiritual influence in it, but God speaks far more eloquently, powerfully and precisely through the Bible than he does through Coldplay. Rely on Scripture, not a person's lovey-dovey showtunes![4]

Stepping back, I reread this person's words and was saddened that he or she could believe God speaks through the Holy Spirit and have no room for that Spirit singing through Coldplay. I think a lot of Christians do this. We're OK with the goodness of creation—and maybe even human culture—during the week, but it's an intrusion on Sunday.

So when we, as a church, explore how God speaks through culture on Sunday, we sometimes hit a nerve.

When the Metallica event was happening at our church, in between all the inquiries from the media I got several calls from some very upset people. "How dare you bring heavy metal into the church!" "This is not of God." "Aren't you a Bible-believing church?" "Those guys aren't even Christians!"

One of the most interesting of these responses came on our church voicemail. The self-appointed prophet raved about how damnable our actions were. Then, as he was wrapping up his call, he quoted an obscure verse from the prophet Ezekiel. And after that he blew a ram's horn into the phone—three times—and hung up.

I think it was supposed to signal some divine judgment (or maybe he was a hockey fan). On ceremonial occasions the ancient Hebrews blew loud horns called *shofar*s. I'm guessing that's what he was using. It's too bad we missed his call. I can just imagine our office administrator passing it on: "Hey John, there's a guy with a *shofar* on line one."

Later that same day another man called and quoted the same verse from Ezekiel. I don't know if he was in cahoots with Ezekiel Man One, but the coincidence did freak me out. And then yesterday, as I was sitting down to write this chapter, I received another concerned e-mail from a totally different person quoting that same verse: "Disaster comes upon disaster; rumor follows rumor. They seek a vision from the prophet, while the law perishes from the priest and counsel from the elders" (Ezek. 7:26). Maybe it isn't that obscure after all!

Seeing this quote again unsettled me. It's not that I think any of these three Ezekiel-quoters are right. Nor do I believe that our church is heading in the wrong direction. But because what we're doing is still relatively new, and because I know I make mistakes and can also be a little headstrong, it's important that I stay open to my critics. So when three separate people, three different times, all send me exactly the same Bible verse, I'm pretty sure I ought to pause and do a self-check.

I have my routine for these occasions. I've done it a hundred times before and since. I go over the story again, usually in the form of a conversation with God:

> I do believe that you made everything, God, and that it all belongs to you. I know you care deeply for every part of this world, especially us human beings, and I have no doubt that you reveal yourself to us stereophonically, through both the Bible and creation.

> I also know that you equip all people with the capacity to hear and see you. You've built it right into who we are, into what we yearn for and desire, into each of our senses. And I believe that who we are reflects something of who you are. Everyone reflects your image in unique and wonderful ways. And when I look around with the right eyes at people, I see reflections of you. You have built your creative power and energy into us, which then become evident in the things we create. Some can see you clearly in all of these things (because they know you personally), and others less so (because they've yet to be formally introduced).

> With all of my heart I believe that my calling as a human being, and our calling as a church, is to help people know and experience you more. I'm convinced that for me, one of the best ways to do

that is to recognize and celebrate where you're already active in people's lives: in the people who surround them, through the things they love, in their playful passions, and in all those other places where they find significance.

I believe that you have led me to see that deep meaning thrives in all those places because you put it there, and you *are* there. God, I have this passion to probe and understand the significance of your presence in all things and to discover it more and more in my own life. I want to share this with others—people inside and outside of the church. We are all made to know and enjoy you, God, and I believe that *all* the goodness, creativity, beauty, joy, and love in this world reflect your glory.

Then God responds and clearly says . . .

Well, that's the problem, isn't it? God hasn't given me his verbal stamp of approval. I've yet to read any definitive writing on the wall. And so I continue to pray that I've got it right, or at least mostly right.

Once I get it all straight in my mind, I keep on trudging. And yes, it still feels like trudging sometimes. Even with as much joy as I have found in this way of engaging God's world, it's still hard work, and it's sometimes quite painful.

Objections from Within

If all of the pushback aimed at me and my church was as over-the-top as what I got from Ezekiel Man, or the man who once stood up in church and called me "Satan's spawn" while I was talking about the theological meaning of poker, or some of the less restrained YouTube commentators, it wouldn't bother me much. But when the concern comes from the inside, from those who are close, who've been longtime community members—people you love—then it's much tougher. I can't just walk away from that, and I don't want to. I want to sit down and talk it over. I want to listen and learn.

Several times during those early years, we had emergency meetings in which we invited the whole community to talk over what we were doing and where we were going. Through those heated discussions, I've come to realize that people's concerns tend to revolve around one of two issues. For some the apprehensions are purely theological—is what we're doing true to the Bible and to the Christian tradition? For others the anxiety is more psychological—it's the inner discomfort many people experience with any kind of change and innovation.

I've also noticed that people often mix the two up, cloaking their psychological unease in theological garb. They think, "I don't feel right about what's going on here, therefore it must be theologically wrong." When that happens, I try to help them distinguish between the psychological issues and the more important theological ones. But on the critical questions—"Is this right? Is this true to God's revelation?"—I want to discuss the legitimacy of what we're doing. I need to do that for the balance and correction it offers to me and to our church community.

In one such discussion, a longtime member who was struggling deeply with how his church was changing said, "OK, I can wrap my head around the idea of God speaking through this book of creation. But it seems that you always read from the same *pop culture* chapter, John. What about the other chapters in God's creation book?"

A brilliant observation. I wasn't preaching from the whole book of creation, and I needed to. So in the months and years that followed I began to explore the whole library of God's glory in creation and human culture. I preached from chapters on architecture, physics, medicine, social science, and the psychology of travel. I'm not sure I ever would have gone there were it not for this person's insightful comment.

At another meeting someone asked, "Why bother looking at creation and culture for God's revelation when we've got this perfectly good source of divine truth in the Bible? After all, isn't the Bible difficult enough to wrap our heads around? Why complicate things by adding this other text? Why not stick to the basics?"

That, of course, gets to the heart of the matter. It's because I know the Bible and have spent years deepening my understanding of it that I am more likely to recognize God in his creation and the reflection of God's image in human culture. So I reminded the group that each week I hold two books in my hands: the book of Scripture and the book of creation and culture. I try to show how *both* books "co-illuminate" each other, how the two voices interacting with each other magnify God's truth.

Perhaps I don't always get the balance right, but isn't it worth the effort? Some people aren't convinced it is, and I can see their logic. The moment you start talking creation, you stop talking the Bible. But I resist that logic and the dichotomy it creates. If God is in every corner of his creation, then are we confronting God *more* when we talk about him from the pages of the Bible than when we talk about him in the intricacies of physics or the pounding lyrics of an angry rock song?

Of course, it's more than a matter of careful balance between the two books. Without the authoritative and inspired revelation of the Bible we'd have great difficulty understanding how God reveals himself throughout creation and culture. That does not mean that we must then "stick to the Bible" as the only meaningful text in which to know God and God's ways in the world. Accepting the Bible's unique authority invites us to open our eyes to see God's glory, love, judgment, and truth all around us.

But Isn't It All Subjective?

There's another problem people have often pointed out with my approach. "I find this whole thing so utterly subjective, John. It seems to me that this entire endeavor of finding God's truth in culture depends very much on what *you're* seeing in these cultural products. That seems very dangerous."

Subjectivity. What place does my personal opinion have next to the divine, objective truth of Scripture? Christians know from historical experience that subjectivity can lead to relativism, which can then lead to heresy.

Usually my first response to this kind of thinking is to engage in a bit of delicious sarcasm: "You're right. It is very subjective. Thank goodness we never have this problem with the Bible!"

We do, of course, have this problem with the Bible all the time. How can we not? When it comes to reading God's Word—in the Bible or in the world—there's always going to be subjectivity when *you* are the one interpreting the text. It's always part of the deal. Human engagement with God's truth, wherever it is found, always involves subjectivity. Theologian Richard Middleton says that the truth doesn't reside in the text itself, it presents itself in that middle place between the reader and the text.[5] We discover truth embedded in the dialogue, in the interaction of the community and the text. And that's true for creational texts as well as the biblical text.

In his book *Velvet Elvis*, Pastor Rob Bell points out that in the Jewish synagogues of Jesus' time, the Torah (the Hebrew Bible) was always read in community. Together the community discerned the meaning of the text as each shared their subjective understanding. Bell argues that we should be doing the same when we read the Bible today.[6]

I believe we should also do the same when reading God's voice in creation and culture. Which is why, more often than not, sermon preparation at our church happens in groups—little modern-day synagogues—sitting down together to listen to and discern the truth in Neil Young's music or a van Gogh painting, as that truth reverberates with the biblical text.

Communal discernment tempers some of the dangers of subjectivity. Together we stay true, or at least stand a better chance of it.

Recently I preached a message on the Coldplay song "Viva La Vida."[7] When I first listened to it, I felt I was hearing the first-person words of Christ's Spirit singing through its lyrics. The hope-filled joy of "I hear Jerusalem bells a-ringing/ Roman cavalry choirs are singing" lifted my spirits with their vision of a made-new Jerusalem. "Be my mirror, my sword and shield/ Missionaries in a foreign field" seemed to echo Christ's Great Commission to his church. The sad admission "I know St. Peter won't call my name" evoked in my imagination Rembrandt's famous painting of the disciple Peter denying Christ, even as Christ is being prosecuted in the background. And with the spiritually renewing and turbulent words "It was a wicked and wild wind/ Blew down the doors to let me in/ Shattered windows and the sound of drums/ People couldn't believe what I'd become," I felt personally blown away by the power of the Spirit. I could just imagine how shocked and astonished Jesus' followers were when the Holy Spirit blew Jesus' power and presence among them on that first Pentecost day.

My personal interpretation of that song seemed so utterly clear to me—until I started getting feedback from my sermon research team.

While a few saw some of the connections I was making, several also got different messages from the song.

This disparity of interpretation initially disturbed me because I thought I'd nailed it. I thought my subjective discernment process was definitive. What I really wanted was to control the song's meaning as I discerned it. I wanted all of the freedom and authority that comes with such exciting subjective engagement. I wanted what seemed so grippingly true in my personal experience of the song to also prove true for others.

As unsettling as this feedback was, it clarified a growing realization that maybe a song *can* and *should* mean one thing for one person and another thing for someone else. It's like a beam of light hitting a prism and refracting into all the individual colors. What if we're experiencing God's manifold brilliance when he disperses truth in this very subjective way? What if this is God's way of engaging every unique individual where they are? Perhaps God is speaking through "Viva La Vida" to millions of souls in millions of different ways at millions of different times.

Rank relativism? Or does all that subjectivity serve God's ultimate purpose?

In an incredibly diverse world of individuals, human subjectivity works brilliantly in two directions. Each person hears God in his or her individual consciousness, and each one also exists as part of the whole community of persons to which and *through* which God speaks. In this way, God's voice, God's truth, is magnified rather than merely atomized or relativized.

It Takes a Community

But there's far more to the communal aspect of seeing God in the whole of creation and culture than tempering the dangers of subjectivity. One of the most exciting parts of this whole endeavor has been its impact on the hearts and lives of people in our church. When you start to connect the deeply resonant creational texts of people's lives to the texts of Scripture, people come alive to the process. It's happened in all kinds of different ways.

When I announced that I was preaching a sermon on seeing God through disabilities, a man with schizophrenia excitedly approached me and proceeded to tell me about all the ways he was recognizing God through his condition.

As part of the preparation for a sermon on the life and music of Johnny Cash, a group of fans came to my house to do message research. First we watched the biopic *Walk the Line.* Then together we worked on the outline for the message. One of the sermon researchers came up to me a week after that meeting and enthusiastically inquired, "When can we do that again?"

A few years back an engineer told me about an architect he'd been studying. He was excited about how this designer's ideas powerfully complemented and illumined his understanding of God's creative planning of space and structure.

When a residential designer heard that I was planning on preaching about architecture, he suggested that he design a house on his CAD (computer-aided design) system during the service. That same week an urban planner told me I needed to read two books he'd studied in university.

Over the past several years, dozens of the messages I've preached have come by request. People in our community watch a film or hear a song or read a book and then challenge me to do a sermon on it. Their passion is invigorating. It's what makes it possible for me to do this kind of preaching. Like the wind, God's Spirit blows where it wills and through whom it pleases. And in the end, we are all exposed to more of the creational text.

When we preached Bach, I got an e-mail from a classical pianist saying she'd love to help me exegete (read into and understand) God's movements in his music. Another woman in the church had already put me in contact with her former music professor in Edmonton, who wrote his thesis on the topic. This woman was so excited. She saw God's fingerprints all over Bach's keys!

The stories go on and on; the community of God searching out, exegeting, and writing messages about God.

And I'm coming to realize that it's critically necessary. In order to preach the creation text we need an army of exegetes; all specialists who practice their passion. I don't know enough about biology or basketball. I need the whole community (the church and beyond) to preach these kinds of sermons.

I needed a major league baseball pitcher and a Pepperdine University kinesiology professor to properly exegete the anatomy of a fastball (all of the power comes from the pitcher's waist and hips, by the way). Professional photographers Freeman Patterson and Galen Rowell (through their books) mentored me in the art of seeing through a camera lens. A beekeeper (apiarist) taught me about the honeybee's amazing and mysterious GPS system (which works kind of like the Holy Spirit does). The stories really do go on and on. When you consider the size of the text you're engaging, it would be impossible for any one person to engage it all.

How exactly do you go about reading the entire world? There isn't a seminary around that can teach you all you need to know. In fact, all of the professors in all of the universities in all of the world would still fall short.

Which is very humbling and exciting.

The whole community works together to answer the question, "Where is God at work in this?" And they, in being asked to engage the question, expand their vision of God in the world. People at our church often talk about how I've "wrecked" movies for them. They no longer watch a film just for entertainment; now they constantly find themselves asking, "What are you saying here, God?" When you acknowledge that God is speaking everywhere, you're forced to engage in seeing and listening more discerningly, and to ask the right questions.

Culture *and* Creation

A lingering question persists: Does God really speak through culture as well as creation? Most people, it seems, can accept the concept of God speaking through the natural world through mountains, oceans, and ecosystems. Doesn't Psalm 19 sing of how the "heavens declare the glory of God"? The hard questions arise when I go beyond the natural world and start talking about movies and art, science and music. The thinking goes something like this: "The natural world displays the handiwork of the creator. Human culture only reflects the often broken and even evil intentions of sinful human beings. How can I hear God's voice in both?" Some detractors concede that human beings may themselves reflect something of the Maker (they are made in God's image, after all), but to claim that God speaks through *the things they make*—that's going too far.

I don't think so. The biblical teaching that God created human beings in his image is an incredibly rich and complex concept. On the most basic level it says that we reflect something of who God is. Historically, theologians have variously defined this *something* as our capacity to reason, to think abstractly, to love, or to live in community.

But there's more to it, because people do more than just reason, think, love, and do community. The stamp of God's image includes *all* of the diversity that is embodied in *all* of the activities of *all* of humanity, in *all* its unique richness. It would take a world full of people, all doing different and amazing things, to even begin to reflect the image of God.

Think about what you do best, or one character trait or natural ability that makes you uniquely you. Now consider the fact that God made you that way on purpose. That good thing in you is God's image built into you (Genesis 1:26). Your athletic ability, your aptitude with numbers, how you're able to plan things, your creative mind—they all come from God.

Writer Dorothy Sayers thought that our capacity to create is *the* first and foremost way in which we reflect God's image. Our expressions of creativity display the core of what it means to image the God who made us.

> How then can [man] be said to resemble God? Is it his immortal soul, his rationality, his self-consciousness, his free will, or what, that gives him a claim to this rather startling distinction? A case may be argued for all these elements in the complex nature of man. But had the author of *Genesis* anything in particular in his mind when he wrote? It is observable that in the passage leading up to the statement about man, he has given no detailed information about God. Looking at man, he sees in him something essentially divine, but when we turn back to see what he says about the original upon which the "image" was modeled, we find only the single assertion, "God created." The characteristic common to God and man is apparently that: the desire and the ability to make things.[8]

So maybe God's image-bearing revelation should be *most sought out* in the creations of human culture.

Writer Tom Beaudoin suggests that it is precisely as imagebearers that we make cultural products, and therefore those cultural products also, to some degree, reflect God's image.[9]

If God's image shines through our very humanity, doesn't it make sense that it also shines through the things we do and make? Of course, sin warps every human activity, but that does not eradicate the stamp of God's likeness in human culture. Even the human capacity to sin reveals God's image in humanity. We can sin and rebel because God did not create us as puppets on strings, but as real individuals with a real capacity for both good and evil.

If all truth is God's truth, and all beauty is God's beauty, then certainly all great guitar riffs are God's great guitar riffs, and all great scientific truths are God's truths. All truth in all of creation, including humanly created culture, is God's truth.

God's truth is so powerful and pervasive that it resonates through everything it touches; through nature *and* human nature.

The Ongoing Journey

These questions—about how the Bible fits into all of this, the place of our personal subjectivity in engaging God's truth, and the whole idea of God's image reflected in human culture—continue to shape our community. We haven't explored all the questions yet, but those we have explored only serve to reinforce and deepen our vision. It has been a difficult but ultimately exciting journey.

This journey may not be for everyone, but to me it's irresistibly compelling and beautiful: searching for the resurrected spirit of Jesus Christ speaking everywhere—in a songwriter's heart and in a runner's legs. Christ in front of us, Christ above us, Christ below us, Christ behind us, and Christ beside us on whatever road we walk.

A Bible story I've been reading illustrates, for me at least, my own journey of discovery. In chapter 24 of his gospel, Luke tells the moving story of two of Jesus' disciples dejectedly returning home to their village of Emmaus. It's after the crucifixion but before they hear the news of Jesus' resurrection. Suddenly Jesus himself joins them on their journey, but they don't recognize him.

Here they are, walking along with the resurrected Jesus Christ right beside them, even conversing with them, and they have no idea who he is. Luke explains it this way: "They were *kept* from recognizing him" (v. 16).

Kept? Kept by whom? By God? Or by the blindness and deafness of that sin virus? Maybe it was all of these. Perhaps God left them in their blindness for a little while. Who knows? Regardless, the situation is intriguing and a bit unsettling. Apparently people of earnest faith— remember, they were Jesus' disciples—can walk through life with Christ right beside them, speaking to them, and still have no idea.

As they walk along, Jesus asks them what's been going on, as though to nudge them into a recounting of the story of his death, a recounting that seems more poignant with Jesus there but not yet recognized. His actions are instructive. It's as though he wants to teach us that the only way anyone can fully understand what they're reading (in the Bible) is to recognize that he's there, right beside them, speaking to them.

The disciples in the story tell him all about the terrible events that took place in the last few days, and the death of the one in whom they had placed all their hopes and dreams.

Then, in what must have been one of the most mesmerizing speeches ever, Jesus explains what had really happened with their hoped-for Messiah. He reframes their old Bible stories into a brand new story, one that fits with a dying and then risen Savior.

When they finally arrive at home, Jesus seems about to move on, but they invite him to share a meal. As Jesus goes through the familiar motions of breaking bread and serving it to the disciples, they suddenly get it. And then, just as suddenly, he's gone.

Once a seminary professor came to me after I'd given a talk on our church's vision. He said, "I think I see what you are doing. I've spent my entire life connecting the Jesus of the New Testament to the Jesus of the Old Testament. You are connecting the Jesus of the New Testament to the resurrected Jesus today."

Yes. That's what I'm trying to do. And that's why I find the Emmaus story so inviting.

Those two disciples didn't have the full story. They were missing the next chapter, and without it they couldn't really understand the chapters that came before. But who could have ever imagined that the plot would take this kind of twist? A death and then a resurrection! No one could see that coming (except a few inspired Old Testament prophets, as Jesus pointed out). And so Jesus lets them in on that continuing story. Joining them on the road, where they were, Jesus reveals that he has now entered that astounding next chapter in God's ongoing story. Jesus shows his followers that those past stories and experiences can't fully explain him, or contain the fullness of who he has now become. It's as if he's saying, "I'm not just *that* Jesus. I'm *this* Jesus, the Jesus who is Lord of history, the one who opens up a brand new future, the one talking to you right now."

That's who Jesus is—God with us right now.

The Emmaus Road story helps me frame the vision for what we're doing in our church: retelling the old story in the presence of the risen Jesus who walks right beside us in our time and place and culture.

8 COMMON GRACE AND *THE DARK KNIGHT*

"You thought we could be decent men in an indecent time. . . . you were wrong. The world is cruel. And the only morality in a cruel world is chance. Unbiased. Unprejudiced."[1]

—Harvey Dent (Two-Face) to Batman, *The Dark Knight*

"This is what God does. He gives his best—the sun to warm and the rain to nourish—to everyone, regardless: the good and bad, the nice and nasty."

—Jesus, Matthew 5:45, *The Message*

"The profane is not always the antithesis of the sacred, but sometimes the bearer of it."[2]

—Frederick Beuchner

If Jesus really is walking with uswhy don't we experience his presence more?

Maybe we're more unconscious than we think. Perhaps sin *is* that blinding, leaving us ignorant and incapable of noticing. Or maybe we're missing it for other reasons. Missing it because we don't dare to believe this kind of story *could* be true, missing it because we've bought into another illusory tale.

You See What You're Looking For

Last year I read a news story about the discovery of yet another dinosaur species; a pint-sized raptor called *Hesperonychus Elizabethae*. Prior to its unearthing, nobody knew this species even existed. Few had even imagined it. Commenting on the odds of anyone making such an exciting find, University of Calgary paleontologist Nick Longrich commented, "You see what you are looking for."[3]

Last month I was reading Alain de Botton's *The Art of Travel*. In one chapter he noted that a person can go through his or her whole life hearing a particular word and never really noticing it, until one day they discover its definition. After that, they hear it everywhere.[4]

Recently I've been looking to buy a used Toyota Rav4. Now I find that I see that model everywhere, as though it's the most ubiquitous car on the road.

You see what you're looking for.

For years I'd bugged our local newspaper editor to let me write an "un-news" editorial. Frustrated that most of the news, day after day, year after year, was downbeat and pessimistic, I had an idea that I should write a piece about how "right" everything was.

What would the news look like were we to report on the opposite story—the flip side of the all-too-negative front page? For years the editor brushed off my idea as ridiculous. But then a new editor took over, and the following editorial was published in the *Calgary Herald* on September 30, 2007.[5]

Mass school shooting . . . man stabbed downtown . . . Category 5 hurricane approaches coastline . . . bridge collapses . . . housing market teeters . . . brand new Airbus crashes . . . child abducted . . . polar ice melting . . . suicide bomber attacks . . . mother dies in fatal automobile accident north of the city. . .

Is it any wonder anxiety rates are on the rise? But should they be? Are things really that bad? Are our fears really rooted in reality? Or are we simply allowing artificially imported, hyped and induced anxieties to disproportionately define and detract from our lives?

It seems that the media thrives on fomenting fear.

It's their job to keep us informed, right? Problem is, nowadays we get the news from every angle, everywhere, all the time! There's no way to avoid it.

This reality is skewing our psyches. What's wrong is being totally blown out of proportion, and we're losing our balance. Cue the ominous backtrack and fade in the jarring graphic.

I know that eye-catching news stories need to have conflict. I understand the publishing rationale, "If it bleeds, it leads." But something tells me—something deep inside—that this continual catastrophic consumption pattern is really not all that good for me. This disaster-rich diet is robbing me of life.

And there's a voice inside that says, "Don't let it! Step back for a second and take an objective look at reality. Things are not as bad as they seem. In fact they're actually good; very good!"

Think about it.

While the tragedies of Virginia Tech and Dawson College were heinous and deeply unsettling, last year some 19 million post-secondary students in North America safely attended university or college, according to Statistics Canada and U.S. Almanac 2006-2007. Every day millions of young adults respected, studied hard alongside, and acted in wholly civil ways toward their teachers and classmates.

Recently, I flew to Chicago for a conference—safely! In fact, in 2006, according to the U.S. National Transportation Safety Board, 750 million passengers had safe journeys on U.S. air carriers.

There were 47 fatalities. In the straight-up statistical lingo of the NTSB, that's 16 million safe enplanements per fatality. 99.99999375 percent of the time, pilots executed their expertise, airline engineers and designers did their computations, security personnel did their checks, maintenance crews provided their care, and air traffic controllers guided their flights safely.

In 2005 there were 595,363 highway bridges spanning the United States.

Assuming a very conservative traffic count of 10,000 cars crossing each bridge each day, and multiplying that number by 365 days per year, the total number of safe bridge crossings was 2.17 trillion! (For Canadian stats, divide by 10.) How well structured is that?

In 2003 there were 134 non-parental abductions in Canada—a parent's greatest fear. That same year roughly 7.6 million children were not abducted; they arrived home from school untouched, had dinner with their parents, and slept in safety, according to the Canadian Centre for Justice Statistics and Statistics Canada.

In the year that the Asian tsunami occurred, arguably one of the greatest tragedies of our times; or in the year hurricane Katrina hit New Orleans, approximately three billion people worldwide lived safely in coastal cities and villages (within 200 km of the coastline, according to Population Reference Bureau, 2003).

You get the point.

And I'm not making it to minimize anybody's suffering. The pain and loss of those impacted by tragedy is both immeasurable and inexplicable. For this reason, their suffering should be ours.

But we need to be careful that we don't become co-dependent on the brokenness of others.

We need to guard against the unhealthy tragedy transference that may be occurring. We need to keep our fears in some kind of balanced check.

There's a recent trend in psychology that's offering this same advice. It's called "positive psychology." The gist of the movement is to switch from the continual focus on what's wrong, where things fall short, and instead accentuate the positive and build from there.

It's a strengths-based approach to living.

We're not talking about denying our problems, ignoring suffering, or minimizing humanity's mistakes. It's more about taking what's good and building on that; focusing on it instead (or at least as much). What do we gain from hyped anxiety and learned helplessness anyway?

This way of thinking seems to be taking off in psychological circles, freeing individuals to focus on what's right and enabling that right to grow. It seems that this re-accentuating trend results in a much more optimistic outlook for many lives.

What if we applied this way of thinking on a larger scale?

There is a lot that is very, very good in our lives (and on our planet). Most of the air we breathe is fresh. Most of the streets we walk on are safe. Most of our lives are filled with un-cited goodness and grace.

Perhaps we need to remind ourselves of these facts more often, and re-proportion our perceptions with a fact-based reality check. Life is good for so many of us, most of the time. Look around. It's the biggest un-news story going!

There's an incredibly common grace at work in our world. The world, as it has for so many millions of years, is still spinning on its axis.

Thank God for that, and for everything else that's holding together so well.

I wrote that piece for myself as much as for others. I wrote it because I needed to see things from a different perspective. Too often I've succumbed to the standard accepted worldview that sees everything that's wrong. But when I started to look at the facts, I realized that the standard worldview is wrong.

You see what you're looking for.

News writers, projecting their worries and pandering to our fearful predispositions, tell us what's wrong with the world. Publishers, well aware that advertising revenues are tied to the number of readers, see how well this kind of news sells and keep it coming. And we, the viewing public in the most media-saturated period in all of history, end up being unreasonably shaped by what they tell us.

But it's not true. The state of the world we live in is not as bad as we're making it out to be. Like the article says, this perspective isn't meant to underestimate our suffering. All I'm hoping for is a more balanced perspective: maybe fifty-fifty? Fifty percent suffering and pain and 50 percent goodness and decency? No, that's not right. Things can't be that bad. Maybe twenty-eighty? Or ten-ninety?

Ridiculous? Think about it. Do the math. Add it up. Count everything that's working right at this moment: your breathing, your mind, your pumping heart, your legs, the fact that you have food to eat, people who love you, a roof over your head, a car (or maybe even two).

Draw a line down the middle of a piece of paper and do the pros and cons of your life. Don't miss a thing. Consider the balance. It's hard because we're so conditioned to see the negative realities.

When you work at recounting reality, your perspective will change. You'll have a more balanced view of even the most difficult circumstances. Where the final percentages land, of course, will be different for all us. But I'm convinced that a proper accounting can restore a healthier outlook.

Pain, it seems, is always shouting and demanding to be counted twice. We need to turn the volume down. Which doesn't mean we become complacent and carelessly accede to the reality of brokenness—that would be ungodly! God doesn't want *any* pain, suffering, or shortfall in his world. Neither should we. Where things are wrong, we should be indignant and want to make them right, while still being careful not to lose perspective.

Things are not the way they should be, but they're not as bad as we're often led to believe, either. Come to think of it, maybe that's why we get so shocked when things go wrong. What if the reason pain speaks so loudly is the fact that life is so right most of the time?

I make this seemingly banal point not just because I want to see the proverbial glass half full rather than half empty. The way I see it, if we hold a predominantly negative view of the world, there's less room for the idea of a God who is working in good and positive ways. But if we change our perspective, if we adopt a more balanced and realistic view, we'll end up seeing more of God's goodness in this world.

And then the question might change to, "How can there *not be* a good, ever-present God, given how amazingly wonderful this world is?"

This idea may seem impossibly naïve, but I'm not suggesting we should ignore the tentacles of evil that penetrate into every aspect of our lives. All I'm saying is that goodness is more powerful and more pervasive than evil. Always has been. But we sometimes lose sight of this fact.

One of the basic teachings of the church has been called *original sin*. It seeks to explain why sin and evil are so all-encompassing in human life by tying them to the story of Adam and Eve's "original sin" in Genesis 3. What that term ignores is that sin is not "original" at all. If you read Genesis 1 and 2 first, you realize that it is actually *goodness* that's original. "God saw all that he had made, and it was very good" (Genesis 1:31). Goodness is original; sin is an invasive species, a parasite that can only live off the good creation. As pervasive and powerful as they seem in our world and our lives, evil and sin are therefore always inferior to and weaker than goodness.

If that's true, then the church is wrong in the way it so often approaches the world.

We in the church tend to take a *sin first* approach, and therefore we're perceived as always being *against* things. We confront alcohol abuse and end up being seen as anti-drinking. We condemn Wall Street's greed and end up looking like we're anti-business. But shouldn't it be the other way around? Shouldn't the church be known for the things we're *for*?

Given what we know about the true nature of this world—about who made it and to whom it belongs—shouldn't we in the church be the most positive voice in the world? And given the core defining characteristic of our faith—*grace*, the idea that God *gives* us free, unmerited, and unconditional love through Christ—shouldn't we be the most inclined to be *for* people? If God is *for* us in this most life-defining way, how can we not be *for* others in response?   And wouldn't this be the best way to effect influence and long-term change?   By naming, celebrating, and growing the good, evil will be displaced.

It's All about (Common) Grace

Grace is central to the Christian story. And it's more common than we might think.

More than half a century ago, a theologian by the name of Louis Berkhof defined it this way:

> [The Holy Spirit] restrains for the present the deteriorating and devastating influence of sin in the lives of men and of society, and enables

men to maintain a certain order and decorum in their communal life, to do what is outwardly good and right in their relations to each other, and to develop the talents with which they were endowed at creation.[6]

Berkhof got his idea from the apostle Paul, who proclaimed: "For [God] made a good creation, poured down rain and gave bumper crops. When your bellies were full and your hearts happy, there was evidence of good beyond your doing" (Acts 14:17, *The Message*).

God's goodness surrounds all people. God's truthful light doesn't discriminate; it shines everywhere. And it's shining more brightly and consistently than we realize. It gives life to everything and sustains the entire planet. It's so immense that often we can't see it. Yet, were it to disappear, life as we know it would end and the cosmos would collapse. That doesn't happen—because grace is stronger than evil's chaotic powers. That's the key truth disclosed in the Bible: "The light shines in the darkness, and the darkness has not overcome it" (John 1:5).

A while back I watched the latest Batman movie, *The Dark Knight*, with Berkhof's definition of common grace in mind.

The film displays the workings of common grace with stunning creativity: good restraining evil within Batman—even though he's mostly good—and good restraining evil in the Joker—even though he's mostly evil.

If you have the eyes for it, you can see that the theme of common grace pops up throughout that film. You can see it in the storyline's uncommon depiction of good and evil. Unlike many movies based on graphic novels, the hero of this tale possesses both good and evil within himself. Like all of us, Batman has a dark side, and he struggles to restrain it, to let good win out over evil. On the other side of the good/evil continuum stands the Joker, who, much to our stereotyping chagrin, has *some* truth and wisdom mixed into his predominately evil disposition. You've got to hate it when the bad guy is right some of the time!

If you step back and look at the overall narrative, you find an even more explicit example of common grace (spoiler alert!) in the ferry scene. There are two boatloads of people—one filled with "good" citizens, the other with criminals. Each boat is given an explosive detonator by the Joker; when pressed, the detonator would blow up the other ferry. The Joker sees this as a bit of a social experiment. He's convinced that the "good" citizens of Gotham will soon show their true colors. Only they don't. They can't. Something in their collective consciences mysteriously restrains them. The same thing happens on the other ferry—the one filled with all the murderers and crooks. In a great paradigm-bursting scene, a tattooed man who first appears to be one of the most hardened criminals steps up to a prison warden and says, "Give it to me and I'll do what you should have done ten minutes ago."[7]

Then he throws the detonator overboard.

"[The Holy Spirit] restrain[ing] for the present the deteriorating and devastating influence of sin in the lives of men and of society." Can you see it?

God not only made all of creation, with all of its goodness built in, God also preserves and sustains it by the Holy Spirit. And if you're looking for that goodness, you'll see that it's all around you.

Philosophers use a famous analytical tool called the *habitus*. This idea began with Aristotle and has most recently been written about at length by Pierre Bourdieu. The concept holds that human action is shaped by external social forces much more than we think. Everything that surrounds us subtly yet powerfully influences our every choice. Commenting on Bourdieu's theories, sociologist D. Michael Lindsay writes,

> [A]ttitudes, responses, and even our preferences are shaped by our *habitus*. What we think we freely choose . . . is instead largely selected by social forces . . . our *habitus* pulls us with unseen forces of attraction. We choose food for our meals, artwork for our homes, and clothing for special occasions according to social judgment. We make choices, of course, but they are conditioned by our locations within society.[8]

Reading about Bourdieu's concept of *habitus* made me wonder if this is how God's Spirit might work through common grace. Yes, it appears as though we have free will, and to some extent we do, but this more powerful curbing, shaping, holding force of God's common grace, disguised as *habitus,* still moves us in the right direction, whether we know it or not. Of course, the force of God's common grace is much bigger than mere social, physical, or psychological forces. God's common grace is behind these forces, animating them.

Still, we wonder, if common grace permeates the world, how can things look so grim? Consider how grim it could get.

Imagine a world where nothing is holding back evil, where all hell *does* break lose, where there is no force holding back nuclear trigger fingers. Imagine a place where human consciences cease to hold us back, where the natural sense of right and wrong—the sense of God's law that's written on our hearts—is absent. Can you grasp the horror of that kind of world? Can you then also imagine how big and powerful the force for good must be that now holds that evil back?

The scope of the good that keeps us from this apocalypse of evil is monumental. Perhaps we're only seeing a small sliver of God's common grace goodness in what is just and true and beautiful in the world. But when you consider how bad things could be, your understanding of the true weight and significance of divine goodness grows exponentially!

Perhaps things *are* much better than we know. And they're even better when we step back and consider our minute place in the overall scheme of things. Were we to take a look at God's watch, God's divine timing for creation, would the suffering we've experienced seem negligible, perhaps even imperceptible?

The thought is sublime, and its possibility points to an almost unimaginable goodness. I doubt we're even close to grasping the good that God has prepared for his creation.

9 "WE GOT TO LET LOVE RULE"

"We got to let love rule. . . ."[1]

—Lenny Kravitz

"Everyone who loves is born of God and experiences a relationship with God. The person who refuses to love doesn't know the first thing about God, because God is love—so you can't know him if you don't love."

—1 John 4:7-8, *The Message*

"To the pure, all things are pure, but to those who are corrupted and do not believe, nothing is pure. In fact, both their minds and consciences are corrupted."

—Titus 1:15

Our church does a lot of strange things on Sunday mornings, but one especially stands apart.

It was late fall 2004, and we'd invited Canadian fashion designer Paul Hardy to debut his spring 2005 collection at our church (before either of his shows in New York or Los Angeles!).

The service began with a full-on thirty-minute fashion show complete with a two hundred-foot runway that ran from one end of our gymnasium to the other, seating for five hundred, video cameras and fashion photographers, spot lighting, live techno music, and twenty top Calgary models from *Mode Models* who donated their time. It was a fabulous event! Local media promoted it and fashionistas from all over the city were in attendance.

The plan for that morning was to start church with the runway show. After that, I would interview Paul Hardy for about half an hour as the sermon. Then I'd pronounce the closing blessing and we'd be done. For the most part, things played out as planned, but I've learned over the years that the real insights cannot be planned for.

For me, the most stunning moment that day was when the congregation, initially seated facing each other on either side of the runway, stood up and turned their chairs ninety degrees to face the church stage. With the simple turn of a chair, the world of fashion morphed into the world of faith. Everyone then sat there, waiting for the message, waiting for some kind of take on where God is moving in the world of high fashion.

In our sermon/dialogue Paul Hardy and I talked about a lot of things; about how God made human beings to be noticed and appreciated (ultimately by God), and how our yearnings for personal beauty and even perfection, at a very deep and intentional level, have been built into us by the God who made us perfect, and will one day bring us to perfection again. And yes, we also discussed some of the perils and excesses of the industry.

I firmly believe that the gospel was preached through the world of fashion that day.

At one point while I was speaking with Paul he did something that deeply moved me. Describing a particular fabric that he had chosen for one of his designs, Paul reached over to the model who was standing onstage wearing the piece, took an edge of the garment in his hand, and described how it was made. Tenderly he detailed the unique weaving process that had been used to create the material, and then went on to explain how the cloth was dyed in India and assembled and cut in a precise way. He knew every tuck and seam. You could tell by his attentiveness and by the tone of his voice that he loved this garment that he had created—in a way only the designer could love it.

Watching Paul, I thought, "God, you must feel the same way when you consider all that you've made."

So I spontaneously shared with the congregation and visitors that Paul's love for his fabrics and garments reminded me of God's particular love and care for everything he created, including us. As I spoke those words to Paul, I had the distinct sense that God was communicating this divine care to all of us: Paul and me and five hundred people sitting in the gym that morning.

God knit us together in our mothers' wombs.

How God must love *all* the creatures he designs—right down to the tiniest detail.

Everything came from God's unfathomable mind. The cosmos was conceived in his heart. Humpback whale tails and black-fly eyes, the Milky Way and subatomic particles, all bear God's fingerprints. Pediatric cardiologists and commercial plumbers, politicians and circus gymnasts, each one lovingly crafted, each reflecting God's creative genius. God thought each of them up. God knows where they came from and his divine design establishes their value.

What inestimable worth this confers on every creature!

And yes, of course, as our maker God also sees the flaws. More than anyone, God is aware of his original intent and agonizes when his creatures fall short. Still, God's love for the creatures he's made is not diminished by their stains and blemishes. Overall the fabric of creation is still good and beautiful.

It's not that God merely overlooks our flaws or sees them through some kind of gauzy veil of heavenly bliss. God, like any artist, is the ultimate perfectionist. God cannot abide the sin that effaces his creation any more than fashion designer Paul Hardy would allow a flawed garment to be paraded down the runway.

God will fix the problem of sin, not overlook it. The Bible tells us the lengths to which God's love goes to restore the torn and stained fabric of his creation.

God looks at all that he has made, takes serious note of the flaws, and works to correct them. But he never loses sight of the beauty of the overall pattern and design.

Because we are made in God's image, we also have the capacity to see the world as God sees it; to love as God loves. When we do, we're able to recognize the goodness of the original pattern. And we're much closer to seeing and experiencing God as the original designer.

This is what happens when a person sees with eyes of love.

Philosopher Søren Kierkegaard, in his commentary on the apostle Paul's phrase "love believes all things," says that only a heart filled with love can truly know and value another person. It's the kind of love a parent has for her child, a love that is able to see the greater good, a larger truth, in spite of constant human brokenness. It's a love that doesn't lose sight of the beauty of an earlier, pre-*fall into sin* time.[2]

Vincent van Gogh expressed the same idea when he wrote, "I think that everything which is really good and beautiful—of inner moral, spiritual and sublime beauty in men and their works—comes from God, and that which is bad and wrong in men and in their works is not of God, and God does not approve of it. But I always think that the best way to know God is to love many things. Love a friend, a wife, something—whatever you like—you will be on the way to knowing more about Him."[3]

Love has a mysterious, revealing, seeing power. I'm not totally sure how it all works, but I do know that it works. I've experienced it.

And when you start to love in this way you'll also discover that a strange synergy starts to play out. As you look at things with love, they become more loveable.

Recently I read an article about a famous herpetologist named Dr. Leslie Anthony. It includes Anthony's description of the scene when, early in his career, he was bitten by a six-foot long boa constrictor: "As I stumbled backward with my free hand on its neck, blood gushing from a stylish, U-shaped needlepoint of some 80 wounds, it actually started chewing—walking its moveable jaws across my arm to inflict new and deeper bites." Eventually he staggered to a sink where he held the snake's head under cold running water until it let go. The attack did nothing to dissuade the young snake lover. He went on to spend the next eight years of his life becoming a herpetologist. "He says he found collecting rattlesnakes and tree vipers 'thrilling, life-affirming, adrenaline producing.' . . . He feels such a strong connection to the animals he sometimes tears up when he spots one in the wild."[4]

Captured by this story, I wondered, "Who loves reptiles like this?" God does, of course. God designed each one of those boa teeth along with every inch of its lethally constricting body.

Which makes me realize how Dr. Anthony embodies this one unique facet of the love of God.

It's often said that a world full of human beings, people from every tongue, tribe, and culture, all together, most fully represent the image of God. Only the fullness of humanity in all of its cultural diversity could begin to capture and reflect the fullness of God.

This makes sense to me, but reading about Dr. Anthony made me wonder if the idea needs to be expanded. This herpetologist obviously shared in God's huge heart for snakes, and that made me think that a full reflection of God's image cannot be limited to humanity's cultural and ethnic diversity. It also has to include the *capacity to love* that is built into each of those people. It would take a whole world full of creation-loving hearts to even begin to reflect God's creation-loving heart.

Perhaps you have seen the Discovery Channel commercial in which expert researchers—climatologists, structural engineers, ocean biologists, archeologists, meteorologists, geologists, entomologists, and more—sing about their love for the world. Stunning visuals depict the breadth and majesty of the creation (starting with two astronauts looking down on the earth). The commercial brilliantly uses real researchers, science nerds, math geeks, and various obscure PhD types to sing the words of the song. As we hear them sing in very ordinary off-key voices, we get a sense of just how much they love what they love.

> I love the mountains, I love the clear blue skies
> I love big bridges, I love when great whites fly
> I love the whole world and all its sights and sounds
> Boom-de-ah-dah, Boom-de-ah-dah,
>   Boom-de-ah-dah, Boom-de-ah-dah!
>
> I love the ocean, I love real dirty things
> I love to go fast, I love Egyptian kings
> I love the whole world and all it's craziness
> Boom-de-ah-dah, Boom-de-ah-dah,
>   Boom-de-ah-dah, Boom-de-ah-dah!
>
> I love tornadoes, I love arachnids
> I love hot magma, I love the giant squid
> I love the whole world, it's such a brilliant place
> Boom-de-ah-dah, Boom-de-ah-dah,
>   Boom-de-ah-dah, Boom-de-ah-dah![5]

While it's not the way we might typically perceive them, I'm convinced that most scientific researchers do what they do because they *love* what they're studying.

And you've got to believe it's their love that enables them to see and understand the intricacies of God's designs in everything from a handful of dirt to the speed of an expanding universe. It's their love that drives them to look so hard, to patiently persevere, to keep hoping and trusting that they'll finally see what they need to see and take that next great step of discovery.

One of the things that moves me in this commercial is the way it sings not only of the goodness in the natural world but also the goodness of the things humans make: bridges and cities, commercial fishing industries, speed racers, rock concerts, fireworks, BASE jumping, and lab research. There's much to love in the nature of structural and physical forces, the tension and compression within a bridge design, the atomic intricacies of radiocarbon dating, and the chemical makeup of fire retardants. By paying loving attention to these physical realities, people honor the deep wisdom and sheer goodness of the Creator.

And it gets better. Were we to study how physicists do their seeing versus how archeologists do their seeing, I think we'd be able to learn even more about what it means to see in general and to see God specifically. Each discipline has something to teach us through its unique method of discernment. Physicists see differently than archeologists. They don't just look in a different *direction*, they look in a different *way*. What would it mean to become a student of these different ways of seeing?

I became that kind of student when I read a terrific book called *On Eloquence* by New York University professor Denis Donoghue. An expert in literature, Donoghue has a keen eye for eloquence. As I read his book, I could sense the deep love he has for words; for their beauty, truth, and elegant articulation. I found myself wanting what he had: both his love and his ability to discern. I wanted these things because I believe that God is the most eloquent being conceivable, the greatest artist and the best writer. And if I want to better understand what God is saying, I need to increase my *eloquence quotient*. The more I know about how eloquence works and what it looks like, the more ability I have to discern God's words.

Halfway through Donoghue's book, I read a few lines of poetry that grabbed me. They were from Philip Larkin's poem "The Trees":

> The trees are coming into leaf.
> Like something almost being said.[6]

When I first read these words, my heart leapt. The idea of a leaf in bud communicating a concept as subtle as the almost-being-said-ness of reality made me think about how all of God's creation is now pregnant with this truth.

Beneath the surface of our present reality, God's glory is waiting to burst forth, patiently bound up but soon to magnificently unfurl. It's all there already, and one day it will be there in its fullness. On the surface, life may seem quite ordinary and seemingly inconsequential—in bud—and yet the potential in it is profound. And to think that it's all there in a budding leaf! Philip Larkin must have spent some time loving and listening to those trees, waiting for them to whisper their eternal truths.

Because of the unique way God gifted him, Larkin was able to listen in a way that you and I wouldn't—or maybe couldn't. Then he eloquently, and again uniquely, described what he saw, so that you and I could see it too. We need Larkin's poetry to help us see the message of a leaf in bud. His love of nature opened his eyes to this message, and his love of eloquence enabled him to express it.

It's All about the Love

The further I go on this *seeing God in creation/culture* journey, the more I grow to love God's world and everything in it. I used to be afraid that if I loved too much, my love would be spread too thin. Not anymore. I'm convinced that I'm supposed to love widely and deeply, and that if my love finds its source in God's heart, I don't have to worry about it running out.

Sometimes it seems strange, this creation-loving stance. After spending so much time listening to and learning to love artists like Metallica, Neil Young, and Amy Winehouse, I find I have them on my heart. Maybe that's an inevitable consequence of operating out of God's heart for his world. For the past two years the love continues to grow. I've been falling in love with physics, with the origins of language, and with redwood trees. Seems I'm becoming a hopeless romantic.

But I've realized that not everybody feels this whole-hearted love for creation. Sometimes people can be quite shortsighted and stingy with their love. This is a huge impediment when it comes to hearing and seeing God's voice in the world.

What makes me say this?

I've seen it in our church. People tend to love what comes naturally to them, and most have limited time and patience for anything beyond that. Often an individual in our community will choose to *not* attend a given Sunday service and say to me, "I didn't come because I'm *not* into fashion . . . or the sub-prime mortgage mess . . . or Barack Obama . . . Rembrandt . . . Coldplay . . . the Olympics . . . biology . . . or Bach. . . ." My first response is, "It's not about the fashion, the sub-prime mortgage mess, or whatever. It's about God." And after I walk away from the conversation, I think, "If they only loved the topic, they'd be so much closer to seeing the God who loves it too, and they'd want to be there."

And when they do love it, they *are there*, physically and wholeheartedly. I've noticed that when I preach on something that people already love, they make sure to make it to church that Sunday, and they invite their friends. I don't like this "pick and choose" trend, but I understand it. It makes me realize that those who already love the particular creational lens we're looking through on a given Sunday are best positioned to get the *God through creation* concept.

A listener who loves Bach has already wondered about that "amazing something" they've experienced in his great compositions long before I preach the classical master. They may never have articulated the experience of the music in spiritual terms, but deep inside they've felt it, this transcendent movement in their souls. I'm convinced that those who already love Bach, who love his music, are halfway there in terms of seeing God behind this genius composer.

And Bach brings them there brilliantly, using a God-given ear and an exceptionally eloquent compositional capacity. Because Bach is so articulate with the language of music, he crafts a beautiful composition. And those who already love his work and understand his language get it.

I was never much of a classical music fan until I preached a Christmas sermon series on J. S. Bach. Then I fell in love.

There was one point, in one of my talks, when I let Bach do the teaching. We were trying to wrap our heads around the mysteries of Christ's incarnation—the idea that Jesus was fully God and fully human at the same time. I could have used words to try to explain it, but words didn't seem big enough. Better to let Bach's music—a different kind of language—preach the point. In his "Credo," where the words of the Nicene Creed affirm that Jesus is both God and human—Bach weaves two voices together, an alto and a soprano singing over and through and around each other, brilliantly depicting the true nature of Jesus' birth.[7] That point could never have been made as eloquently with words. The mystery of the incarnation needed a different language—music, in this case.

Bach cannot say all there is to say about God through the language of music, but perhaps he can say *best* what certain parts of God's truth might feel like, or sound like—those parts that only music can communicate through its unique ability to engage our emotions. This kind of knowing should never be construed as a complete knowing of God. Like words, music has its limits. As one writer put it, "You can convey emotions with music . . . but you cannot make a dinner appointment or a train reservation without words."[8]

Capturing all that God is saying takes all of the myriad forms of human endeavor, from musical notes to eloquent words, from electron microscopes to handling snakes, from sports to politics, all engaged with loving attentiveness.

None of us can love it all the way God does; that would be impossible. But we can learn to love it more. And perhaps the passions and loves of others can teach us and spur us on. Certainly God's love for all things should.

Love brought the universe into being, and love sustains every moment of it. It's therefore only through our loving attention to this world and everything in it that we'll be fully able to engage and experience God's love there.

10 A CHILDLIKE IMAGINATION

"A child in the cradle, if you watch it at leisure,
has the infinite in its eyes."[1]

—Vincent van Gogh

"I'm telling you, once and for all, that unless you return
to square one and start over like children, you're not
even going to get a look at the kingdom, let alone get in.
Whoever becomes simple and elemental again, like this
child, will rank high in God's kingdom."

—Jesus, Matthew 18:2-4, *The Message*

"We begin with the capacity to learn more effectively
and more flexibly about our environment than any
other species. This knowledge lets us imagine new
environments, even radically new environments. . . ."[2]

—Alison Gopnik

I have a friend named Lillian. Even though she's in her seventies, she's younger than me. She is so alive and she always seems to be laughing out loud. Every time I talk with her, she's brightly attentive and exudes this wonderfully genuine sense of *joie de vivre*. She refuses to act her age. When I see her this way, she reminds me of God.

Writer G. K. Chesterton once wrote, "It may be that [God] has the eternal appetite of infancy; for we have sinned and grown old, and our Father is younger than we."[3]

Chesterton's remark reminds me of a beautiful scene I witnessed recently in a cataract surgeon's waiting room. I was sitting there with my wife, who had received a brand new artificial lens in her right eye the day before. She, along with a roomful of elderly folks, was there for her post-op check-up to have the bandages removed. A nurse would call each person into an examination room, remove the plastic shield and dressing that covered his or her eye, do a quick test, and then send the person back to the waiting room to wait for the doctor.

So there I was, sitting in a room full of newly sighted seniors. What I saw was profound. Wide-eyed and filled with wonder, an elderly Italian man sitting straight across from me, a Dutch woman named Willy seated just beyond him, and a frail Hmong man to my left were all looking around the room like three-year-olds. You could tell they were seeing more clearly than they had in years.

I wondered what it would take for me to undergo that same transformation. I felt envious and also a bit cynical. How long would it be before they'd grow old and forget that they'd received new sight?

Have we lost touch with how to see with childlike eyes?

Our capacity to be amazed and to wonder at the unfolding cosmos often seems to diminish with age. We don't look behind, beyond, and beneath things as much; nothing surprises us anymore. We've grown old, and our imaginative vision fades along with our cataract-clouded eyes.

This malady, this loss of our childlikeness, is a huge impediment to seeing God in the world. Our lost innocence deadens our senses.

Dr. Hans Rosling teaches a university course called "Global Health" at the Karolinska Institute in Sweden. His classes are filled with the brightest young minds in the country. Before beginning his course, he likes to get a general idea of what his students already know about the subject. So he gives them a simple pre-test. Projecting the names of five pairs of countries onto the overhead screen he asks, "Which country has the highest child mortality of each of these five pairs?" Just to be fair, he's set up the test so that in each pairing, one of the countries has twice the child mortality of the other.

The final result? The students average 1.8 out of 5 correct answers. Initially Rosling was a bit perplexed when he realized that the top students in Sweden knew significantly less about the world than a chimpanzee would—statistically, the chimp would have gotten it right at least half the time.

Dr. Rosling realized that the problem with his students lay not in their ignorance but in their preconceived notions. What caused the students to be more wrong than right was what they *thought* they already knew.[4]

This happens all the time. It happens in communities, countries, companies, families, and churches. Not that there's anything wrong with thinking you already know something. We can't go through life as though everything is brand new. But we have to be very careful about *how much* we think we know. We need to know things, while realizing at the same time that we really don't know much at all, and that there is still so much more to learn.

Children are naturals at *knowing things* this way.

They're young enough and still humble enough to realize that what they know isn't everything there is to know. Of course, none of us ever really knows that much, relatively speaking, yet we tend to lose touch with this grounding perspective. We lose this healthy humility of childhood.

We think we know how God works. Or we think we've seen all there is to see of God in life. We go to church, sing a few songs, help at the local soup kitchen, read the Bible once in a while, and think we know something. We settle for what we *think* we know and, by doing so, leave little room for a greater knowing. Maybe it's because we've never experienced God in ways other than the narrow confines of our own lives.

But what if God is new every day?

Writer Madeleine L'Engle once observed that Jesus' mother, Mary, "was little more than a child when the angel came to her; she had not lost her child's creative acceptance of realities moving on the other side of the everyday world. We lose our ability to see angels as we grow older, and that is a tragic loss."[5]

You know that's true if you've ever witnessed a young child who is filled with awe at something new. The fact that we're caught by the child's excitement and even vicariously enter into it says a lot about us. For me these moments always come with the realization that I rarely feel this way anymore.

I love it when I get in touch with those long-forgotten feelings through a child, but I love it more when I experience them for myself. I often pray for God to keep me young at heart. I don't want my ability to see God to diminish. I want my imagination to stay awake.

Realizing I don't know anything about God right now, relatively speaking, is a good start. I need to appreciate that in *God years* I'm only an infant, and always will be. If that seems too hard to swallow, simply put what you think you know next to what God knows, and you shouldn't have a problem. It's part of becoming like a child.

Like the writer of Psalm 103, imagine your life filled with a renewed sense of carefree wonder: "He wraps you in goodness—beauty eternal. He renews your youth—you're always young in his presence" (v. 3, *The Message*).

In recent years my camera has been helping me see like a child again. Something about a zoom lens opens my eyes wide. Enlarging my view of everyday objects invites me to become engrossed in the details once more. When I hold my camera at oblique angles, I'm able to see from a new perspective. And as I try to frame images, I'm more cognizant of what's filling my viewfinder. I notice how things are juxtaposed, how they talk to each other. It's as if my camera makes me young again—and even when it's not with me I find myself noticing details and nuances in light, texture, and shape.

This is a huge gift. Often I'll get completely lost in my subject, totally absorbed by what I'm seeing—just like a child. Surely God means for me to see this way, with this kind of heart. Once Jesus called a child over and said to his disciples, "I'm telling you, once and for all, that unless you return to square one and start over like children, you're not even going to get a look at the kingdom, let alone get in. Whoever becomes simple and elemental again, like this child, will rank high in God's kingdom. What's more, when you receive the childlike on my account, it's the same as receiving me" (Matthew 18:2-5, *The Message*).

In Jesus we see a model of what it means to grow up without growing old. Jesus was childlike with his whole being, while at the same time he was fully mature. He was young enough to hear his Father's voice and playfully announce the kingdom of God in the ordinary stuff of everyday life: flowers and weeds, losing and finding. Jesus' childlikeness fully fit with his grown body and mature mind.

I want to live in that elemental childlike place Jesus calls me to.

The other day I was listening to a radio talk show interview. Alison Gopnik, a psychology professor at the University of California, was talking about her new book, *The Philosophical Baby*. As she spoke about a child's amazing capacity to enter into other worlds and to interact with imaginary friends, I couldn't help but remember Jesus' call to participate in a kingdom that is *here but not fully here*. It seems to me that this same ability is critical for knowing that a Holy Spirit invisibly walks with me and leads me into a new world.

In her book, Gopnik writes that children are mysterious and, therefore, are closer to and more at home with mystery. Children's amazing brain plasticity—"the ability to change in the light of experience"—allows them to process change at an incredible pace. Because a baby's brain—especially the prefrontal cortex—is immature, levels of inhibition are much lower than in adults, leaving the child "open to anything that may turn out to be the truth." Babies fully engage in and receive parental love— they do not grasp the risks, of course—and that love equips them to imagine, to learn, and to grow.[6]

In our church, I've noticed that the young and the young at heart are often the ones who most deeply resonate with the idea of God revealing himself in the world. They are wide-eyed enough to think it could be true, open-minded enough to trust, and imaginatively attuned enough to see.

I once preached a series of messages based on famous children's stories, hoping they would resonate with the childlike. My desire was for all of us to grow younger as we engaged familiar imaginative tales like *Pinocchio* (a God who makes wooden people real[7]), *Green Eggs and Ham* (taste and see that God is good), *Finding Nemo* (a modern day prodigal son), and *Are You My Mother?* (asking the two big existential questions: "Who am I?" and "Are you my mother?"). The children were certainly fully engaged for that month of Sundays, but so were the adults.

"For my part," wrote nineteenth-century British poet and novelist George MacDonald, "I do not write for children, but for the childlike, whether of five, or fifty, or seventy-five."[8]

I believe God communicates the same way.

Our challenge is to reengage our imaginations and listen accordingly.

Reimagining

I often wonder if our God-given ability to imagine—what children do naturally—is *the* discernment tool for apprehending and engaging God's mysterious movements in the world.

When you consider that God made this world out of *his* imagination and that God created us with the capacity to imagine, doesn't it make sense that this faculty, more than any other, might be crucial for our ongoing relationship with God? It makes sense that God gave us imaginations so we could experience all that he's imagined, in a way that only our imaginations can grasp. Imagination, it seems to me, is the place where the *created* and the *Creator* meet, where the material encounters spirit.

In an article called "The Wise Imagination," Trevor Hart writes:

> One of the key tasks of the imagination, [George MacDonald] tells us, is to clothe invisible spiritual realities with material forms, enabling us to grasp them more securely. This is what the poet does, for instance, when he refers to love as "quick-e'yd," (George Herbert), to resentment "keeping its wrath warm" (Robert Burns), or to the Spirit of God brooding over the world with "warm breast and . . . bright wings" (Gerard Manley Hopkins). When ideas take flesh in this

way, MacDonald suggests, words are duly born anew of the Spirit.[9]

Where else but in our imaginations can the Mystery at the center of the universe meet us mortals? Perhaps it's the only faculty that's open-ended enough, timeless and spaceless enough, creative enough, out of our control enough, to receive all that God has for us.

In my own experience, it's usually my imagination that opens the door to seeing God in creation. And it's *within* my imagination that I unwrap the revelatory gift, play with it, and more fully comprehend it.

Here's what happened in my imagination when a sermon on Ray Charles first came to mind.

I was out for a walk, listening to Ray sing with the Count Basie Orchestra—*Ray Sings, Basie Swings*—and enjoying an absolutely stunning sunshiny day. It wasn't hard to feel like I was a kid that day. Everything seemed new. Listening to the first tune on the album, "Oh, What a Beautiful Morning," my imagination quickened.

The song is bright, bouncy, and filled with hope: "There's a bright golden haze in the meadow/ The corn is as high as an elephant's eye/ And it looks like it's climbing clear up to the sky/ Well, oh what a beautiful morning/. . . I've got a beautiful feeling/ . . . Everything's goin' my way/ . . . The sounds of the earth are like music."[10]

As I was listening to the words, taking in the beauty of the day, I wondered if God sang something similar when he first called the cosmos together; rejoicing at the sheer goodness of what he'd just made. "God saw all that he had made," points out the writer of Genesis 1, "and it was very good."

But the Ray Charles song ends—at the very last chord—with a bit of dissonance, on a slightly flat note, with this barely perceptible but undeniably clear sense of the ominous: "Nothing to worry about." But there is!

The next few songs on the album give evidence of harmony shattered. There's rebellion ("Let the Good Times Roll") and adultery ("How Long Has This Been Going On?"); signs of the fall seem to be everywhere. People are going their own way and turning their backs to God instead of their faces.

Listening to the lyrics of "Crying Time," I wondered if God felt that way as he looked down on his wayward world: "Oh, it's cryin' time again, you're gonna leave me/ . . . I can see that far away look in your eyes."[11]

We all know those "cryin' times."

And yet there are still hopeful moments in the song, a hanging-on kind of hope: "Well, my love for you can never grow no stronger/ If I lived to be a hundred years old."

God couldn't forget his covenant with us; his deep and abiding promise to never stop loving us.

The next song in Ray's musical narrative, "I Can't Stop Loving You," affirms this fact. And in "Come Live with Me," we really see the heart of God:

> Come live with me and won't you be my love
> So I can love you all, all the time
> Be part of me, well, be the heart of me
> Be mine[12]

Of course all of these songs were written about a man's love for a woman. Or were they? For centuries theologians have been debating the meaning of a steamy scriptural work called Song of Songs. Is the passion articulated there really about the love between a man and a woman? Or is it about the love between humanity and God?

I'm thinking, why can't it be both?

Surely the love shared between a man and woman is analogous to the love we share with God. And God's love informs and infuses the love that we share with one another. The intimate nature of the love that Ray Charles sings about is a lot like the nature of God's love for each of us. Didn't the apostle Paul refer to the church as Christ's bride? Didn't Jesus talk about making a place for us with many rooms? And aren't we all called to be a part of him, the heart of him? The redemptive love in these songs is so beautiful, so moving. I feel like God is singing them to me.

"Be mine."

And then the album wraps up with Ray singing the Beatles ballad "A Long and Winding Road." It's all about the journey, about returning, about finding that door, the way back home.

> Why leave me standing here
> Let me know the way
> Many times I've been alone
> And many times I've cried
> Anyway you'll never know
> The many ways I've tried
> And still they lead me back
> To the long and winding road
> You left me standing here
> A long, long time ago
> Don't leave me waiting here
> Lead me to your door.[13]

And then—I couldn't believe my ears—Ray ends his version of the song with the powerful doxology "Amen."

Amen—so let it be. It was perfect.

My imagination ran wild with the thought of it—all those biblical images of Christ running through my head: a door, a way, a road home. Jesus promising not to leave us behind, assuring us that he'd come back to us by his Spirit and come back for us one day. It was a moment filled with God's presence—and all through a Ray Charles album my daughter brought home from Starbucks one day.

Throughout the entire walk it felt like God was singing to me, and I was singing back. After all, I'm made in the image of a singing God.[14] I felt the tone of God's voice as I imagined his joy at creation. I sensed God's emotion in the hurt that resulted from my turning away.

And then the theologian in me took over. I stood back and realized that the central storyline of the Christian faith—creation, fall, redemption, and return—was also captured in the juxtaposition of these few songs.

Can you imagine that? Are you young enough?

Did God plan for all of this to come together the way it did? After all, God did create Ray Charles in his image, didn't he? Maybe Ray couldn't help but compile this album in this way. It was built into his life story, scripted, and yet it freely emerged from his own imagination.

That's the idea that keeps floating around in my head. I've got a picture of God holding all this in his providential hand in a very planned and purposeful way, God knowing it would all fit together so beautifully, and the Spirit's mysterious energy behind it all—animating, shaping, and leading. It was all God's idea in the first place. I just happened to trip on it.

Trip on it. That's what it felt like. The way you'd feel if you were six years old and found a quarter on the sidewalk. Like it was a great treasure. Pure serendipity. You couldn't ever plan on finding something as great as this. It was just there: you picked it up, examined it, and stuck it in your pocket.

"Everything of man must have been of God first," said George MacDonald. "So what the poet 'creates' he really only 'finds.' The patterns are already present in the mind of God, awaiting our discovery."[15]

Coldplay's Chris Martin says much the same thing: "The bad songs come from me and my knowledge of how to write songs, and the good ones come from somewhere—I have no idea where. And they tend to be sort of flying around at about two o'clock in the morning. You just have to be there to catch it. That's how I feel about the good ones."[16]

So many artists share this sense of discovery. To consider that all truth is already there, awaiting our imaginative grasp, is the ultimate game-changer for me.

We think this way all the time in relation to the nature of our physical world. When two Nobel Prize-winning physicists—Albert Fert of France and Peter Grunberg of Germany—*independently* discover an effect called "giant magnetoresistance" in 1988 (a development that allows iPod hard disk technology to exist) we have no trouble believing it was there before they found it. This reality-shaping magnetic effect existed and was mysteriously at work long before 1988. The same applies to Newton's discovery of gravity and the discovery by Einstein and others that light is both wave and particle at the same time.

There are physical realities at play all around us that lie beyond our awareness and scientific principles yet to be discovered—even as they exert a huge influence over our lives.

If this is true in the physical world, why couldn't it be true in a broader sense as well, like for a thought, a tune, a story? Why wouldn't God be imperceptibly moving behind all things in ways that are yet to be discovered?

Doesn't God call us to believe in the unbelievable, to see unseeable things, to catch them as they fly by? And isn't faith really only possible with the help of a very active and engaged imagination? The courage to believe beyond evident possibilities, despite the weight of logic?

Aren't we supposed to see faces in clouds?

Only our imaginations can make the necessary room for the impossible; living into another kingdom, seeing an invisible God moving in the world, hearing an inaudible voice from an invisible friend, knowing the incomprehensible mystery behind all things.

God imagined reality as we know it. God created us with imaginations so that we would have the capacity to mysteriously perceive him in this created reality. And then, in an astonishing display of divine hospitality, God invited our capacity to imagine into the ongoing story of the universe. God freely included us as co-creators, co-imaginers, and co-authors. And somehow through this imaginative collaboration, the best narrative is being written; God's perfect plan is playing out.

In *The Mind of the Maker*, mystery writer and essayist Dorothy Sayers writes of the deep joy a playwright feels in watching her script brought to life by the actor.

> To hear an intelligent and sympathetic actor infusing one's own lines with his creative individuality is one of the most profound satisfactions that any imaginative writer can enjoy; more—there is an intimately moving delight in watching the actor's mind at work to deal rightly with a difficult interpretation, for there is in all this a joy of communication and an exchange of power. Within the limits of this human experience, the playwright has achieved that complex end of man's desire—the creation of a living thing with a mind and will of its own.[17]

Imagine the joy God feels in inviting you and your imagination into his story!

God invites all of us to play a role in his collaborative and redemptive production. In order to fully participate, we need to muster every bit of childlike creativity and imaginative energy we've got. We need to study the script, read it well, and then, with innocent abandon and trust in God, throw ourselves into the part—just like you did when you were a young child listening to your mom, dad, or grandparent read you that story, hanging on every word. Do you remember how it felt? Sitting so close as she reads to you; so free to enter into the narrative. A whole new world became alive to you. You went places and did things you could have never imagined. This is what it means to enter into and believe in God's bigger story. This is what trust in a nearby Narrator can bring to your life, no matter how old you are.

11 PARABLE EARS AND ICON EYES

"Do you not know? Have you not heard? Has it not been told you from the beginning? Have you not understood since the earth was founded?"

—Isaiah 40:21

"There's more to the picture than meets the eye."[1]

—Neil Young, "Hey Hey, My My (Into the Black)"

"I . . . wrestle with nature long enough for her to tell me her secret."[2]

—Vincent van Gogh

W hat if Jesus is still preaching parables today? New ones. For our times.

Sometimes I wonder if all of the creational, truth-filled stories that are now playing out in our world are exactly that: the resurrected Christ, through his Spirit, continuing to speak in the same way he always has—through parables.

In the New Testament gospels, Jesus used parables as his primary method of communicating God-truth. In these short, earthy stories he connected the ordinary things of day-to-day life with the extraordinary realities of what he called the kingdom of God.

In a single chapter of the gospel of Matthew alone, Jesus pictured the kingdom through stories of a farmer, seed, weeds, gravel, a bad neighbor, soil, trees, yeast, buried treasure, trespassers, jewel merchants, pearls, fishnets, and a general store owner (ch. 13).

"Why all the stories?" his disciples asked. And Jesus responded,

> You've been given insight into God's kingdom. You know how it works. Not everybody has this gift, this insight; it hasn't been given to them. Whenever someone has a ready heart for this, the insights and understandings flow freely. But if there is no readiness, any trace of receptivity soon disappears. That's why I tell stories: to create readiness, to nudge the people toward receptive

insight. In their present state they can stare till doomsday and not see it, listen till they're blue in the face and not get it. I don't want Isaiah's forecast repeated all over again:

> Your ears are open but you don't hear a thing.
> Your eyes are awake but you don't see a thing.
> The people are blockheads!

> They stick their fingers in their ears
> so they won't have to listen;
> They screw their eyes shut
> so they won't have to look,
> so they won't have to deal with me face-to-face
> and let me heal them.

But you have God-blessed eyes—eyes that see! And God-blessed ears—ears that hear! A lot of people, prophets and humble believers among them, would have given anything to see what you are seeing, to hear what you are hearing, but never had the chance. . . .

Are you starting to get a handle on all of this?

—Matthew 13:11-17, 51, *The Message*

I certainly want to!

I'm beginning to think that all of the modern-day creational parables I'm experiencing are a kind of parable in my own life, born out of a Spirit-created readiness in me that is nudging me toward receptive insight. It makes me wonder if those who first listened to Jesus' parables experienced the same sense of epiphany I feel every time I meet God in creation. Is this what it feels like to hear one of Jesus' parables—*live*?

And I wonder about the nature of parables. What is it about these stories that makes them the perfect carriers of mysterious kingdom truth? Why did Jesus choose this particular genre? If I understood better how they work in me, would I be able to hear more clearly?

"A Catch of the Breath"

"It is the mark of the good fairy-story, of the higher or more complete kind," J. R. R. Tolkien once wrote, "that however . . . fantastic or terrible the adventures, it can give to a child or man that hears it, when the 'turn' comes, a catch of the breath, a beat and lifting of the heart, near to (or indeed accompanied by) tears, as keen as that given by any form of literary art."[3]

It seems to me that Tolkien's words apply equally well to parables as they do to fairytales. I can imagine Jesus' listeners experiencing "a catch of the breath . . . a beat and lifting of the heart . . . tears." I can see their jaws dropping and their eyes shining. The power of Jesus' parables always seemed to reside in that mysterious *turn*:

- So then the Samaritan—from the wrong side of the tracks—*risked his life* to save the injured man . . . (paraphrased from Luke 10).

- And then the rejected father of that good-for-nothing prodigal son *ran* to greet his rebellious returning boy . . . (paraphrased from Luke 15).
- At the end of the day, the vineyard owner paid the slothful, late-coming workers a *full day's wage* . . . (paraphrased from Matthew 20).

Talk about surprising turns!

Jesus' parables stunned people, shook them out of their complacency, snapped them to attention. He spoke God's truth with a new kind of authority. Those who heard it couldn't help but be moved—or angered—by it. They knew something more was going on.

And I wonder if that *something more* is the same as the something more that I experience in the *turn* moments of the stories I encounter today:

- And then the whole town, even though they knew that Lars was a little crazy, put their common sensibilities aside and lovingly went along with his ridiculous delusion. For his sake they became fools . . . (paraphrased from the film *Lars and the Real Girl*).
- But then Remy, the rat turned chef, proved the stereotyping food critic wrong—proved all those judgmental souls wrong—when he showed him that rats *can* cook, and that you should never be quick to judge things unclean that God has made clean . . . (paraphrased from the animated film *Ratatouille*).

- So then Walt Kowalski, an ill-tempered old man, confronted the evil gang, but instead of engaging them in a shootout, he let them kill *him*. When his neighbors saw this sacrifice, they were shaken out of their complacency and cowardice . . . (paraphrased from the film *Gran Torino*).

In each of these stories, there's a twist that takes our breath away. And in that vulnerable and surprising moment, a new world of understanding opens up. When we hear Christ's words in his parables, we suddenly come face to face with who we really are, who Christ is, and where we came from.

There's something about how these surprising turns work. When the turn is a note of grace, our necks crane, our hearts leap, and we experience a sense of *This is the way love should always be*, a sense of *Wow!* Who could imagine a heart that would so willingly embrace a prodigal son? Who could ever envision a nasty neighbor like Walt making that kind of selfless sacrifice? This kind of love, we know, has only one source: the heart of God.

But there are other kinds of turns as well—equally compelling, but coming at us from a different direction. Not all of Jesus' parables—past or present—focus on grace. Some are reminders of judgment. In these, the turn comes in the form of a dreadful surprise: *Oh no!*

- And then those blind-to-the-hidden-Christ goats got sent to an eternal fire . . . (Matthew 25:31-46).

- But no sooner had the successful rich man built bigger barns to store all his stuff than he died in his sleep . . . (Luke 12:13-21).
- Suddenly the high rollers in that God-fearing Western society got the economic shock of their lives . . .

Judgment parables affirm that God is holy, and not to be messed with!

In other parables the turn evokes a deep sense of incomprehensibility and mystery. So, for example, when Jesus said that the kingdom of God—the most magnificent state of reality conceivable—was like a mustard seed or like yeast, it would have elicited still another kind of response: *What?* Modern-day versions of this kind of parable might be found in the study of quantum mechanics, deep space exploration, or nanotechnology. Explore these texts and you'll be left with *otherworldly* mysteries beyond imagining. God's kingdom is unfathomably mysterious.

The fact that parables (past and present) come in these different forms—grace, judgment, and mystery—has been an important discovery for me. When I first started reading creational texts, I'd spend a lot of my time looking for the *good stuff*. I'd cherry-pick God's readily apparent—clearly on the surface—goodness, grace, and truth wherever I could find them. Not a bad thing, of course, but limiting in terms of fully engaging parables of judgment or the mysterious parables of the kingdom. I've since learned that not all of Jesus' parables—in the Bible or today—speak of love and grace. Some are hard hitting, others incomprehensible.

So when I try to see, hear, and read what Jesus is saying today, I need to remember that parables come in different forms, and each of these parable types works in its own way. What's common to all of them is that surprising turn. When we experience the turn in a parable—whether it's through the *Wow* of grace, the *Oh no* of judgment, or the *What?* of the mysterious kingdom—we experience God's love, God's authority to judge, and God's mysterious wisdom.

Writer Frederick Beuchner talks about how prophets, when they speak their truth, "do not say something as much as they make something happen."[4] This must be what happens when Jesus, *the* prophet, speaks in parables. Through a gracious, judging, or mysterious turn, Jesus turns our faces toward him. We see his point in the story, but more important, we see *him*.

Everyday Epiphanies

By using common, everyday sights and experiences in his stories, it's as though Jesus intends to seed our minds with the possibility of a God who speaks everywhere. Each of these everyday stories can become a touchstone for recalling and experiencing God's real time, right now presence.

Can you imagine a life full of these everyday, ordinary epiphanies?

Parable enthusiast and scholar Robert Farrar Capon wrote that the key to understanding parables *isn't* in making the right interpretation of what Jesus said. Instead, he said, we need to hang Jesus' words on the "walls of [our] mind," whether we fully understand them or not, and let them act as icons.[5]

I love this image. Our minds are like art galleries in which God hangs his parabolic truths. These icons speak to us in the same way art speaks to us. Not overtly, not primarily with logic or reason, but tangentially, on a slant, with beauty, emotion, and subtle suggestion.

This is what artists do. They craft their works, in part, "to create readiness, to nudge the people toward receptive insight," just as Jesus does with parables (Matt. 13). We experience them as much as we logically interpret them. "God does not sign his sunsets . . ." writes Frederick Buechner, "nor does he arrange the stars to spell out messages of comfort."[6] He doesn't have to. Creation speaks its own language—many different languages, in fact. We just need to translate them.

Of course, God does speak more directly to us at times through commandments, prophecies, wise advice, and historical action. Often God's logic shines with the clarity of the legal system or the way the laws of physics define the structures of the universe. But not all of creation is penned in legalese or described in natural laws.

Parables are just as true as these more directly discerned realities, but they communicate their truth in a different, more story-like way. People who have trouble understanding biblical parables or modern-day parables often hold to a purely rational, moralizing form of thinking. Of course, parables do contain logic and reason, but these elements always serve the larger message of the story.

Interestingly, Jesus didn't tell just one or two parables, but dozens, and who knows how many more that were never recorded. He made sure that the minds of his listeners were fully stocked with a gallery full of these iconic stories. To me this makes perfect sense. Because the mysterious workings of God's kingdom could never fit into the frame of a single parable, Jesus presents the many facets of the kingdom through all kinds of jewel-like masterpieces.

Parables work together. Even as our imaginations invite us to enter each individual story, there's something about having another story nearby, the one behind you to the left and the one on the other side of the gallery. Together they collectively communicate the whole message of the artist. There's a feeling, a sense of the complete story in the room. As our minds are increasingly stocked with these word-images, after we've made a few turns, we find ourselves much closer to the ultimate story: the *kingdom of God* story.

For me, parables operate in a way that is very similar to the icons of the Eastern Orthodox church. While traditional icons may seem like ancient stylized pictures to the casual observer, Orthodox worshipers see them as windows into the reality of God's mysterious kingdom. As they describe it, one does not so much look *at* an icon as *through* it.

In the same way, we do more than just listen *to* parables. We're supposed to listen *though* them, to hear the startling, unsettling, life-giving message of God's kingdom.

How exactly does this seeing and hearing *through* things work?

Writer Madeleine L'Engle describes the nature of iconic windows this way: "A true icon is not a reflection; it is a metaphor, a different, unlike look at something, and carries within it something of that at which it looks."[7]

When I first read L'Engle's definition I smiled. That is exactly what I'd experienced with my own eyes on a crisp, true blue Rocky Mountain morning while out on a pilgrimage.

On my day off I'd decided to head out to the site of the first church founded in our region: the Our Lady of Peace Mission nestled in the foothills just west of Calgary. I figured a trek to the monument would be a good opportunity to think about God's lasting presence in the region. I wanted to meet God there.

As I walked down a desolate gravel road to the cairn, I noticed something spectacular. The ditches were filled with light! Countless drops of dew—the remnants of a heavy foothills frost—glistened like diamonds. I pulled out my camera, stretched out in the grass to get as close as possible, and took photograph after photograph. And the dew spoke.

Each tiny transparent drop carried within itself "something of that at which it look[ed]," like a lens or a window capturing budding grains of wheat, the surrounding grasses, even an entire mountain range. The definition of an icon was right there in the very nature of each droplet.

> "Who fathers the drops of dew?"
>
> —God to Job, Job 38:28

To me those dewdrops were the perfect picture of an icon's mysterious nature. Hours earlier they were frost, cold and opaque, but in that moment, at just the right temperature and under just the right light, those shining drops came alive. Like a good camera lens, they captured the *beyond*.

The grain and mountains I could see within these droplets were not the real thing—"scents of an unseen flower," as C. S. Lewis put it—but neither were they false images or mere reflections. Because what they were representing was real, they were real in an *unlike* way. Realities that were further away than they appeared in the dewdrop (inches in the case of the grass, miles in the case of the mountains) appeared much closer.

This is what icons can do, under the right spiritual conditions. They bring God closer. They take something inestimably huge and scale it to our human perception.

What if God intended for all of creation to serve in this iconic way, carrying within it "something of that at which it looks"? Can you imagine what that would be like—the entire cosmos acting like a dewdrop, giving us more *through* which to know and love God?

> "Listen, Heavens, I have something to tell you. Attention, Earth, I've got a mouth full of words. My teaching, let it fall like a gentle rain, my words arrive like morning dew. . . ."
>
> —Deuteronomy 32:1-2, *The Message*

The dew became a lens through which to see God, a watery window into God's providential presence, a visible sign of how richly he blesses, sustains, and satiates his world.

If creation is God's greatest piece of art, then perhaps we need to engage it as such, not always expecting only linear, rational, comprehensible revelation but also different, *unlike* ways of knowing. Perhaps we need to accept that knowing God is as much an art as it is a science.

The morning I chose to head out on that dewy pilgrimage (and God chose to show me his lasting presence in the ditch rather than the church monument), a Bible verse I'd read before breakfast was running through my head: "I hear this most gentle whisper from One I never guessed would speak to me . . ." (Psalm 81:5, *The Message*).

Those words set the tone for that entire icon of a day. They became a lens for seeing God, for hearing him. In some mysterious way they introduced those first few dewdrops to me. God's scriptural truth working deep inside me reached out to God's creational truth all around me. The Bible's words gave me permission to expect the Whisperer's presence.

Over and over again I repeated the verse, and as I did, *it* became iconic. My vision seemed to clear and my hearing grew more attuned. And as my awareness of God's presence in the icon of nature grew, the words of the psalm writer became even more transparent.

God's presence seemed to embody the moment:

> *I hear* . . . that's present tense, right now . . .
> *this* . . . not *a* or *the* but *this* . . .
> *most gentle whisper* . . . Jesus is close, very close . . .
> *from One I never guessed would speak to me* . . .
> How could I ever have guessed that *you* would
> speak to *me*? And yet you do.

You come to me.

You came to us, became one of us. You whispered. Before even speaking a word, you simply *were* . . .

> a baby,
> an icon of intimacy,
> a God who lets us hold him.

Jesus certainly carried within him something of that at which he looked:

> I am the way and the truth and the life. No one comes to the Father except *through* me. If you really know me, you will know my Father as well. From now on, you do know him and have seen him.

—John 14:6-7 (italics mine)

> No one has ever seen God, not so much as a glimpse. This one-of-a-kind God-Expression, who exists at the very heart of the Father, has made him plain as day.

—John 1:16, *The Message*

Through the icon of Jesus Christ we are able to see God the Father. He is our door, our window, our dewdrop to the eternal.

Jesus is someone *through whom* people can see God. God reveals himself through Jesus, and he bears God's image perfectly. To be fully human is to be fully alive in both these ways. "I'm telling you this straight," says Jesus. "The Son can't independently do a thing, only what he sees the Father doing. What the Father does, the Son does. The Father loves the Son and includes him in everything he is doing. . . . I can't do a solitary thing on my own; I listen . . ." (John 5:19-20, 30, *The Message*). When human beings live in this wholly dependent and empowered way, they become more iconic.

The closer we are to God, the more transparent—in the best sense of the word—we become.

Jesus lived his iconic potential perfectly. And when we listen to what he's saying through the images and parables he once spoke, and continues to speak, we will know the truth that sets us free as human beings.

This is the goal of human life: to know and enjoy God in this way. To see the fingerprints and hear the voice of the Creator in every corner of the creation.

Jesus understood that the Father is the artist who came up with the design concept in and behind everything that is. Perhaps that's why he was able to weave the mystery of the kingdom of God into an iconic seed: it was already there! Just as you or I might readily identify a certain painting as a van Gogh, or hear a certain song and recognize Bono all over it, Jesus couldn't help but see his Father's genius in all that filled the cosmos. Jesus' complete dependence on his Father and the deep intimacy with which he listened to God's every whisper made that very apparent to him.

This ability to see deeply, to recognize God in everything, is one of the ways in which we understand Jesus' humanity-for-us. Because Jesus lived that way—*as a human being like us*—we know that's the way we're supposed to live. Like Jesus, we live in a world full of parables, a gallery of icons through which we are allowed to see into the depths of reality.

As Jesus himself said, we won't find eternal life, full and abundant life, just by parsing the verses of the Bible: "You have your heads in your Bibles constantly because you think you'll find eternal life there. But you miss the forest for the trees. These Scriptures are all about *me*! And here I am, standing right before you, and you aren't willing to receive from me the life you say you want" (John 5:39-40, *The Message*).

Our ability to live a full and abundant life comes in recognizing the One to whom every word points. Life is in him, in living like him—alive to God in every moment, in every thing, every day.

12 HEAVEN ON EARTH

"There is one timeless way of building. It is thousands of years old, and the same today as it has always been. The great traditional buildings of the past, the villages and tents and temples in which man feels at home, have always been made by people who were very close to the centre of this way. It is not possible to make great buildings, or great towns, beautiful places, places where you feel yourself, places where you feel alive, except by following this way. . . . This way will lead anyone who looks for it to buildings which are themselves as ancient in their form, as the trees and hills, and as our faces are."[1]

—Architect Christopher Alexander

"I am the way. . . ."

—Jesus, John 14:6

"Behold, I am making all things new."

—Jesus enthroned, Revelation 21:5, ESV

We are meant to experience God in all things.

I'm convinced of this.

At every turn, on every street corner, when we get up, when we lie down, and in everything in between, we're meant to see God's face and hear God's voice. We were made for this kind of existence, created with the capacity to sense and experience God in everything, all the time.

This is what it means to be a human being. This is what it means to be fully alive.

It's heaven on earth.

At least the kind of heaven I believe the Bible talks about; the one where God takes this messed-up world and makes it brand new again. The one in which our relationship with God is fully restored and we know him perfectly in all things. Heaven as God's great conclusion.

This notion of heaven on earth makes me wonder about the exciting ideas I've been living with and preaching on over the past few years. Does the idea of seeing God through a film, hearing God through a song, or experiencing God in a stadium, gallery, or classroom *fit*? Do these here-and-now experiences connect with God's long-term vision?

I believe they do. I believe these revelatory glimpses are foretastes of heaven on earth. And what we now know in part, we'll one day know perfectly!

When this heavenly connection first came to me, I breathed a huge sigh of relief. Everything finally started to fall into place and make sense. What has become my deepest conviction, and what we've been doing as a church, is about getting ready for heaven on earth.

God is preparing us for the future through these experiences.

This insight first came to me when I preached a series of sermons on architecture and on the city.

God as Architect

As I began my research on architecture, I asked a few friends to respond to this question:

> Try to describe the most perfect place you've ever been. A place where everything was just right: the view, the way you felt, the way the moment just fit together. What was it like?

Here's what some of them said:

- "The chair by the cabin window looks west toward the foothills. The low-hanging clouds burst over the hill, darting this way and that, while up above, so far above, a sun dog is playing for what seems like an eternity. And for that same eternity, sitting in my window seat, I too am at peace in a turbulent world."
  —Rob

- "I'm about ten years old, lying in a snow cave that has been carved in my backyard . . . a remarkable two-room shelter with a tunnel so tight I can barely make my way through. It is earthy and cold, safe and magical . . . a portal into a world of wild childhood imaginings, a perfect handmade palace. . . . I could hide out here forever!" —Carol

- "Visiting the Capilano Suspension Bridge when I was fifteen, I wandered off the trail and lay down on the soft green moss, smelling the green cedar scent in the warmth, staring up through the green cedars at the green-colored rays of sunshine coming through the treetops. I could feel, smell, and see green—God was completely there and I felt his presence. It was incredibly peaceful and serene. Today if I feel stressed I remember that moment and try to feel, smell, and see it all again." —Barb

- "Disneyland's new park, California Adventure, is like that (alive, true, free, and eternal). No matter where you stand, the geometry and colors are perfect." —James

- "I recall an early afternoon meal shared with my daughters on a cool late-summer's day some years ago in Bryant Park next to the . . . main branch of the New York Public Library. As we ate in this former 'needle park,' we watched children ride the carousel, working folk sitting on the green park chairs with their brown paper bag lunches, a fashion shoot taking place in one of the park's corners, and, suffusing the scene, the dapple of sunlight rippling through the tall, reedy, breeze-blown plane trees. One of my daughters turned to me and said, "This is how I imagine [heaven]." —Gideon[2]

Reading these responses, I found myself wanting to be in those places. I began to imagine a life filled with these perfect spaces, endlessly strung together. Everything *just right,* my heart at peace, my imagination alive, everything around me just as it should be: children playing, a clean world, all things made new.

They're trying to get back to the Garden, I thought. And they're reaching for heaven. This is all about regaining the perfection God intended for creation. The experiences they describe evoke the memory of a long-forgotten past and the dream of a *one day* future.

I wondered if, in each of those timeless, perfect places, these people were mystically experiencing God's perfection—actually getting a small foretaste of heaven.

I'm not talking here about the stereotypical, halo-wearing, harp-playing picture of heaven. I'm talking about the real vision of heaven, the biblical vision. The one in which God makes *all things* brand-new, in perfect harmony, just as it was originally intended to be.

Renowned architect Christopher Alexander wrote about this vision of heaven in his book *The Timeless Way of*

Building. Here's his description of a way of being he calls the *timeless way*:

> Almost everybody feels at peace with nature: listening to the ocean waves against the shore, by a still lake, in a field of grass, on a windblown heath. One day, when we have learned the timeless way again, we shall feel the same about our towns, and we shall feel as much at peace in them, as we do today walking by the ocean, or stretched out in the long grass of a meadow.[3]

Alexander talks about the *timeless way* within the context of the physical design and construction of buildings and urban spaces. One day we'll get our designs so *right* that our towns will feel like a walk on the beach. His urban design vision reminded me of the *sensus divinitatis* and its *just right* feeling—moments and places that are not so much created as discovered, times when we feel perfectly attuned to ourselves and our surroundings, as though everything fits perfectly. In his work I saw the connection between a twenty-first-century architect's dream and that of sixteenth-century theologian and reformer John Calvin.

Alexander's vision was to bring the peaceful feeling that we experience in nature into our cities and towns. He envisioned the creation of "great buildings, or great towns, beautiful places, places where you feel yourself, places where you feel alive." To create physical spaces that embody this kind of aesthetic and evoke this kind of human response is a powerful architectural ideal.

Alexander's dream is evidence of our yearning for heaven. But it's not complete. It's not big enough.

Had the Old Testament prophet Isaiah read Alexander's book, I'm sure he would have smiled in agreement and then whispered, "But there's more!"

Describing God's vision of "new heavens and a new earth" (65:17), Isaiah saw much more than *just* spatial and aesthetic harmony and the good feelings that those kinds of spaces evoke. He envisioned a definition of peace (shalom) that was more expansive than mere bricks and mortar. He saw a shining city that was multiculturally whole; filled with commerce, wealth, and prosperity; governed in perfection; overflowing with justice.

Isaiah's vision differed from Christopher Alexander's in that it filled a perfect *city* with a perfect *society*. A perfect society grounded in a perfect, renewed relationship with God.

> "Pay close attention now: I'm creating new heavens and a new earth. All the earlier troubles, chaos, and pain are things of the past, to be forgotten. Look ahead with joy. Anticipate what I'm creating: I'll create Jerusalem as sheer joy, create my people as pure delight. I'll take joy in Jerusalem, take delight in my people: No more sounds of weeping in the city, no cries of anguish; no more babies dying in the cradle, or old people who don't enjoy a full lifetime; one-hundredth

birthdays will be considered normal—anything less will seem like a cheat. They'll build houses and move in. They'll plant fields and eat what they grow. No more building a house that some outsider takes over, no more planting fields that some enemy confiscates, for my people will be as long-lived as trees, my chosen ones will have satisfaction in their work. They won't work and have nothing come of it, they won't have children snatched out from under them. For they themselves are plantings blessed by God, with their children and grandchildren likewise God-blessed. Before they call out, I'll answer. Before they've finished speaking, I'll have heard. Wolf and lamb will graze the same meadow, lion and ox eat straw from the same trough. . . . Neither animal nor human will hurt or kill anywhere on my Holy Mountain," says God.

—Isaiah 65:17-25, *The Message*

In Isaiah's (God's) world all things will be *just right* again. Everything will fit: honest government always working for the people, more than enough wealth to equitably go around, everyone getting along, a city, a world, at peace. "Then you will look and be radiant," says the prophet, "your heart will throb and swell with joy; the wealth on the seas will be brought to you, to you the riches of the nations will come" (Isa. 60:5).

Can you imagine it?

Isaiah's heavenly city isn't a stark otherworldly contrast to life as we know it in this world. It is a *continuation* of all that's good, true, and meaningful right now. All that's right in this world—politicians who keep their word and lead us to an even greater vision of what a country can be, scientists who continue to discover all there is to know about our amazing cosmos and technology flourishing as a result, entrepreneurs who come up with more and better ideas, citizens who continually respect and care for the environment, athletes who give it all they've got— will carry on in a perfected form. Cultural patterns and societal ways—wherever they fit with God's good will— will make it through to the life hereafter.[4]

The prophet Isaiah saw this future vision of heaven on earth, and the apostle John echoed it in his vision called Revelation. John further fills in the picture in describing heaven as a *city* that will *come down* from God to earth.

> I saw Heaven and earth new-created. Gone the first Heaven, gone the first earth, gone the sea. I saw Holy Jerusalem, new created, descending resplendent out of Heaven, as ready for God as a bride for her husband. I heard a voice thunder from the Throne: "Look! Look! God has moved into the neighborhood, making his home with men and women!" . . . The Enthroned continued, "Look! I'm making everything new. Write it all down—each word dependable and accurate."

—Revelation 21:1-5, *The Message*

What a vision: God in the neighborhood!

The visionary writer goes on to describe this heavenly city as a place with walls and gates built with proportion, beauty, and color. It has foundations that are made of spectacular building materials, an architect's dream! It's a city with a crystal clear river running down the middle of the main street, lined with the most amazing trees, whose leaves are "for the healing of the nations" (Revelation 22:2). It's a city with a perfect balance of aesthetics, design, and green spaces.

This is God's plan. A real city.

God's heart for urban planning with balanced green spaces reminds me of an inspiring talk I recently saw on TED.com. Landscape ecologist Eric Sanderson begins his presentation by saying, "The substance of things unseen. Cities past and future." He had my attention.

Sanderson's goal was to deconstruct New York City, the world's first megacity, and re-create its 1609 ecosystem, hydrology, and geology. Using an old map and "reams of data," Sanderson "re-envisioned, block by block, the ecology of Manhattan."[5] He rediscovered a lost world; a wonderfully diverse, resilient, and interdependent bio-network made up of beaches, wooded heights, meadows, streams, and a wetland (now Times Square). It was a place where wildlife flourished: bears and beaver, timber snakes, fish and frogs, birds and bees. The whole system worked naturally as one.

Then Sanderson overlapped this newly created "Old Manhattan" with the existing city. From this new composite he was able to show us what the Old Manhattan would have been like from any contemporary office building window. It was hard not to long for that nature-filled bygone era! Yet Sanderson didn't stop there. He went on to speak of his love for the present city and its diversity and interdependence. He spoke of the continuity between the two Manhattans. And then he dreamed of the city four hundred years from now. His description brought tears to my eyes.

> So, how can we envision the city of the future? What if we go to Madison Square Park, and we imagine it without all the cars, and bicycles instead, and large forests, and streams instead of sewers and storm drains? What if we imagined the Upper East Side with green roofs, and streams winding through the city, and windmills supplying the power we need? Or if we imagine the New York City metropolitan area, currently home to 12 million people, but 12 million people in the future, perhaps living at the density of Manhattan, in only 36 percent of the area, with the areas in between covered by farmland, covered by wetlands, covered by the marshes we need. This is the kind of future I think we need, is a future that has the same diversity and abundance and dynamism of Manhattan, but

that learns from the sustainability of the past, of
the ecology, the original ecology, of nature with
all its parts.[6]

Remembering a Garden, dreaming of a future City.

All of the lessons from God's originally designed garden
apply perfectly to the city, the pinnacle of human development and culture. As Sanderson described his vision, all I
could see was God's heavenly city—a city the way it was
always meant to be.

Heaven, from a biblical perspective, is all of this—life and
culture and commerce, leisure and sport, art and science
and architecture—made new, redeemed, perfected, and
continuing forever. All that is wrong, perverted, twisted,
and sinful will fall away; all that is good will find its
rightful place.

Heaven is the *reality we now live*—made perfect! Imagine
the earth filled with world-class cities together reflecting
the glory of their Maker. Imagine an unparalleled diversity
of people working as one, all of creation flawlessly bearing
the image of a holy, communal God.

If this is the Bible's take on heaven, then what exactly
are we experiencing when we have our own epiphany
moments: a child in a magical snow fort, a teen enveloped
by green, a man enjoying a theme park?

What is happening when we experience that perfect
moment of physical intimacy with another human being?

When the beauty of a song or a painting or a movie captures our soul? When an architect's aesthetic leads us to seek out a timeless way, or we walk the streets of New York City and catch a glimmer of the heart of God?

Are they all pointers to that future perfect city?

No Temple There

Are all those moments, those *just right* and true times that feel pregnant with God's presence that we sometimes experience in the diversity of a city, in the beauty of a scientific theory, in the oneness of a World Cup soccer game, or in the intricacies of a fabric's weave, heaven on earth? Are they foretastes, moments where God bends time, leans over, and whispers to us, "There's more"?

Is heaven's new earth going to be one continuous, eternal string of these revelatory kinds of events? Everything done perfectly, everything in accordance with God's will, everything clearly revealing something of God's goodness and grace, everything, every action, all that we do, done for God's glory?

Surely the new earth will be a place where God is perfectly experienced and known and loved through all things. All of creation *will be* a perfect icon then. And we'll be able to know and love God in all we do and experience. God will have moved into the neighborhood.

The book of Revelation says that the new city won't have a temple because God will be its temple (21:22). What does that mean?

Church buildings will be totally beside the point in a world where we know God in and through all things as we live every part of our perfect new earthly existence. We'll experience God in the lab, love God on the playing field, worship God at the theater. We'll fall on our knees as God reveals his wisdom through the mysterious design of tectonic plates and unveils beauty through an amazing sculpture. We'll cheer as God demonstrates explosive power through a world-class Olympic sprinter.

This whole *seeing God in creation* worldview we've been exploring is about starting to live this kind of life right now, right here.

It's about heaven breaking out here on earth. It's about experiencing a moment of life the way God meant it to be, knowing God perfectly and then knowing ourselves.

Human Being

When I presented some of these creational revelation ideas at a workshop in Toronto, a woman in the back of classroom raised her hand. She asked, "So, what kind of person do you see being developed by this vision? At the end of this kind of worldview, what would a person look like?"

I thought for a moment and then replied, "She'd look like someone who's learning how to discern, to see and love God in *all things.*"

I wish I could answer that woman's question over again.

What would that kind of man or woman look like?

He'd be the kind of person who, whenever he witnessed goodness in another person, would, without even thinking, see God as the source of that goodness. All that's good, perfect, and true in this world would instinctively turn his heart to God, perhaps even to the point of seeing God behind the person doing the good deed.

This kind of person would realize that everything she does carries God's revelatory potential. She bears the image of God. She's held by and mysteriously led by the Holy Spirit. So when she comes up with a new idea or creates something wonderful, she would recognize that God is speaking through her. Everything in life would take on a new sense of gravity. Things would matter more.

This kind of person would also do everything in his power to grow and develop his listening capacity. He'd read his Bible expectantly, leaning into it as the story that defines and illumines his life today, the story he lives out of each moment.

What else?

This person would love the world the way God does. As she comes to know God through all things, she'll love those things even more. And that love won't just be a sentiment, it will translate into action. A deeper knowledge of God's presence in the world will drive and inspire this person to act, to get in on making all things new.

Finally, this all-encompassing life of faith would give this person an ever-deeper knowledge and experience of God through Christ. He or she would know Christ's love fully and feel totally alive, would know this is what it means to be a human being!

We have no idea how much God wants to reveal himself to us. Nor can we fully imagine the revelatory stops that he's pulled out in order to make that happen.

————

After my sermon series on architecture, a friend sent me an e-mail. She and her husband run a residential design firm, and both were struck by the idea of perfect places and spaces being a foretaste of heaven on earth. Did that mean that when her husband gets a client's kitchen design right—perfectly fitting who that person is, what her needs are, and all the functional requirements of that space—that he is a co-creator with Christ, bringing heaven on earth?

Was God, through them, really bringing *heaven on earth* in a kitchen, through a façade, by means of the right lighting and countertop specification? And to think that they could personally know, commune with, experience, and honor Christ as they did this! Last week I caught the new marketing tagline for their business: *Helping you find your way home.*

Imagine God revealing himself through the way a baker runs her bakery, through scientists' understanding of supernovas, through the way we produce energy, through all the ways we play, through the development of new technology. Imagine God speaking through every activity and substance that fills every square inch of this blessed universe: God at work, creating it all, co-creating more of it through each of us, and then, through everything, revealing more and more and more of who he is.

Imagine God doing this forever, for the rest of eternity (which I'm guessing is about how long it will take for him to fully reveal who he is), and through it all, receiving all of the glory due his name.

It's a powerful vision, emanating from the all-powerful mind of God, redeeming creation from the inside out through the mysterious growth of a brand-new kingdom, a whole *new way.*

It's a huge idea. And it requires great faith and commitment on our part.

We need to dare to believe that Jesus really is who he says he is, that Jesus is enthroned over all creation right now, and that he holds everything together.

So what kind of people would be developed by this vision?

People who realize that what's happening inside their hearts is also happening in all of creation, for *everyone* and *everything* in the cosmos.

People who fall to their knees and join the song: "Praise the Lord, all his works everywhere in his dominion" (Psalm 103:22). "For from him and through him and to him are all things. To him be the glory forever! Amen" (Romans 11:36).

NOTES

Chapter 1

1. James Hetfield, Lars Ulrich, Kirk Hammett, and Bob Rock, "Dirty Window," *St. Anger*, © 2003, Creeping Death Music (ASCAP).

2. Michelle Mark, "Church to Hear Heavy Message: Sermon on Metallica," *Calgary Sun*, May 5, 2004.

3. James Hetfield and Lars Ulrich, "Nothing Else Matters," *Metallica*, © 1991, Creeping Death Music (ASCAP).

4. James Hetfield, Lars Ulrich, Cliff Burton, and Kirk Hammett, "Creeping Death," *Ride the Lightning*, © 1984, Creeping Death Music (ASCAP).

5. James Hetfield, Lars Ulrich, and Kirk Hammett, "And Justice for All," *And Justice for All*, 1988.

6. James Hetfield and Lars Ulrich, "Holier Than Thou," *Metallica*, © 1991, Creeping Death Music (ASCAP).

7. John Calvin (*Institutes*, 1.5.1), quoted in *Engaging God's World* by Cornelius Plantinga Jr. (Grand Rapids, Mich.: Eerdmans, 2002), p. 27.

8. *Calvin: Institutes of the Christian Religion*, ed. John T. McNeill (Philadelphia: Westminster Press, 1960) 2.2.15, pp. 273-274.

9. James Hetfield, from mtvICON interviews, introduction by Jon Wiederhorn, interviews by Erica Forstadt, © 2007 MTV Networks. MTV.com.

10. James Hetfield, Lars Ulrich, and Kirk Hammett, "The Unforgiven," *Metallica*, © 1991, Creeping Death Music (ASCAP).

11. James Hetfield, VH1 interview, "Building the Perfect Beast," Wednesday, June 25th, 2003. http://www.vh1.com/artists/interview/1473275/20030625/metallica.jhtml

Chapter 3

1. Vincent van Gogh, *The Complete Letters*, 197, I, 365, quoted in Don Postema, *Space for God* (Grand Rapids, Mich.: Faith Alive Christian Resources, 1983, 1997), p. 14.

2. Kathleen Powers Erickson, *At Eternity's Gate: The Spiritual Vision of Vincent van Gogh* (Grand Rapids, Mich.: Eerdmans, 1998), p. 97.

3. Erickson, *At Eternity's Gate*, p. 99-100.

4. Erickson, *At Eternity's Gate*, p. 169-170.

5. Erickson, *At Eternity's Gate*, p. 74.

6. Vincent van Gogh to his friend Bernard, *Letters*, 3:495, quoted in *At Eternity's Gate*, pp. 181-182, by Kathleen Powers Erickson. © 1988 Wm. B. Eerdmans Publishing Company. Used by permission.

7. Erickson, *At Eternity's Gate*, p. 171.

8. Erickson, *At Eternity's Gate*, pp. 94-95.

9. Erickson, *At Eternity's Gate*, p. 93.

10. Vincent van Gogh, *Letters*, 1:495, quoted in Erickson, p. 76.

11. Vincent van Gogh's mother in a letter to his brother Theo, *Letters*, 2:230, quoted in Erickson, pp. 91-92.

12. Vincent van Gogh in a letter to his brother Theo, *Letters* 1:268, quoted in Erickson, p. 91.

13. Lyrics from *Les Misérables*, original Broadway cast recording released January 28, 2003.

Chapter 4

1. St. Augustine, *Confessions,* trans. and with an intro by Henry Chadwick (New York: Oxford, 1992), 145 (8.7.17); 3(1.1.1).

2. Cornelius Plantinga Jr., *Engaging God's World: A Reformed Vision of Faith, Learning, and Living* (Grand Rapids, Mich.: Eerdmans, 2002), p. 7.

3. John Van Sloten, "The Flames in the playoffs is like dying and going to heaven, says a Christian pastor," *Calgary Herald*, May 26, 2004.

4. Evanescence, "Bring Me to Life," *Fallen*, © 2003, Wind-up Entertainment, Inc.

5. C. Plantinga, *Engaging God's World*, p. 7.

6. *Calvin: Institutes of the Christian Religion*, ed. John T. McNeill (Philadelphia: Westminster Press, 1960) 1.5.1, p. 52.

7. Alvin Plantinga, *Warranted Christian Belief* (New York: Oxford University Press), p. 175.

8. A. Plantinga, *Warranted Christian Belief*, p. 183.

9. St. Augustine, *The Confessions of St. Augustine*, trans. by Rex Warner (New York: New American Library, 1963), p. 235.

10. C. S. Lewis, *Weight of Glory and Other Addresses* (New York: HarperCollins, 1941, 2001), pp. 30-31.

11. From the website http:/improveverywhere.com.

12. Sean Wilsey, *National Geographic,* June 2006.

Chapter 5

1. From the screenplay of *Crash* by Paul Haggis and Bobby Moresco, p. 96.

2. Michael Becker and Bird York, "In the Deep," *Wicked Little High*, © 2006 Blissed Out Records.

3. These lyrics are a saying attributed to Rumi, a Sufi mystic.

Chapter 6

1. From the screenplay of *No Country for Old Men*, adaptation by Joel Coen and Ethan Coen, based on the novel by Cormac McCarthy, p. 86.

2. St. Augustine, *City of God*, XIX, 13, quoted in Reinhold Neibuhr, *Christ in Culture* (New York: Harper & Row, 1951), p. 211.

3. *No Country for Old Men* screenplay, p. 107.

4. *No Country for Old Men* screenplay, p. 107.

5. *No Country for Old Men* screenplay, p. 122.

6. The Apostles' Creed.

Chapter 7

1. hottamale02, comment on sermon excerpt "The Gospel According to Barack Obama, Part 1: Leadership," YouTube.

2. MrSunshine124, comment on sermon excerpt "Neil Young, God's Prophet?" YouTube.

3. chimmister, comment on sermon excerpt "Horton Hears a Who: Believing the Unbelievable," YouTube.

4. bhamcubfan, comment on sermon excerpt "Coldplay—Knowing God," YouTube.

5. J. Richard Middleton, *The Liberating Image: The Imago Dei in Genesis 1* (Grand Rapids, Mich.: Brazos Press, 2005), p. 38.

6. Rob Bell, *Velvet Elvis* (Grand Rapids, Mich.: Zondervan, 2005), p. 50.

7. Coldplay, "Viva La Vida," *Viva La Vida*, 2008.

8. Dorothy Sayers, *The Mind of the Maker* (New York: HarperCollins, 1979), p. 22.

9. Tom Beaudoin, *Virtual Faith* (New York: Jossey-Bass, 1998) p. 34.

Chapter 8

1. From the screenplay of *The Dark Knight* by Jonathan Nolan and Christopher Nolan, p. 135.

2. Frederick Buechner, quoted in "Flesh and Blood in the Magic Kingdom" by Wendy Murray Zoba, *Christianity Today*, March 2003.

3. Katherine O'Neill, "Tiny Feathered, Meat-eating Dinosaur Discovered in Alberta," *Globe and Mail*, March 16, 2009.

4. Alain de Botton, *The Art of Travel* (New York: Vintage, 2004), p. 183.

5. John Van Sloten, "Obsession with Disaster Is Making Us Miserable," *Calgary Herald*, September 30, 2007.

6. Louis Berkhof, *Systematic Theology*, (Grand Rapids, Mich.: Eerdmans, 1941), p. 426.

7. *The Dark Knight* screenplay, p. 130.

8. D. Michael Lindsay, "The Sociological Two-Way Mirror," *Books and Culture*, March/April 2009.

Chapter 9

1. Lenny Kravitz, "Let Love Rule," *Let Love Rule*, 1989.

2. C. Stephen Evans, "Kierkegaard Among the Biographers: The Hermeneutics of Suspicion," *Books and Culture*, July/August 2007.

3. Vincent van Gogh, *Letters*, 1:198, quoted in Erickson, *At Eternity's Gate*, pp. 66-67.

4. Anne McIlroy, "Fangs for the Memories," *The Globe and Mail*, December 20, 2008.

5. Discovery channel commercial, http://www.metacafe.com/watch/yt-at_f98qOGY0/discovery_channel_commercial_boom_de_ah_dah/

6. Philip Larkin, "The Trees," quoted in Denis Donoghue, *On Eloquence* (New Haven: Yale University Press, 2008), p. 70.

7. Insights into Bach come from Calvin R. Stapert, *My Only Comfort: Death, Deliverance, and Discipleship in the Music of Bach* (Grand Rapids, Mich.: Eerdmans, 2000), p. 93.

8. Charles Rosen, "From the Troubadours to Frank Sinatra," *New York Review of Books*, February 23, 2006, quoted in Donoghue, *Eloquence*, p. 123.

Chapter 10

1. Vincent van Gogh, *The Complete Letters*, 518 III, 2, in Postema, *Space for God* (Grand Rapids, Mich.: Faith Alive Christian Resources, 1983, 1997), p. 28.

2. Alison Gopnik, *The Philosophical Baby: What Children's Minds Tell Us about Truth, Love, and the Meaning of Life* (New York: Farrar, Straus and Giroux, 2009), p. 8.

3. G. K. Chesterton, *Orthodoxy* (San Francisco: Ignatius Press, 1995), p. 66.

4. Hans Rosling, from the website http://www.ted.com/talks/lang/eng/hans_rosling_shows_the_best_stats_you_ve_ever_seen.html.

5. Madeleine L'Engle, *Walking on Water* (Colorado Springs: Waterbrook Press, 2001), p. 10.

6. Gopnik, *The Philosophical Baby*, pp. 4, 8, 13, 15.

7. Neal Plantinga, from a preaching conference presentation at King's University College in Edmonton.

8. George MacDonald, *A Dish of Orts* (Whitefish, Mont.: Kessinger Publishing, 2004), p. 195.

9. Trevor Hart, "The Wise Imagination," *Christian History & Biography*, April 1, 2005 (www.ctlibrary.com/ch/2005/ch/issue86/16.40.html).

10. Ray Charles, "Oh, What a Beautiful Morning" (Rogers and Hammerstein), *Ray Sings, Basie Swings*, 2006.

11. Ray Charles, "Crying Time" (Buck Owens), *Ray Sings, Basie Swings*, 2006.

12. Ray Charles, "Come Live with Me" (Boudleaux and Felice Bryant), *Ray Sings, Basie Swings*, 2006.

13. Ray Charles, "The Long and Winding Road" (John Lennon, Paul McCartney), *Ray Sings, Basie Swings*, 2006.

14. Zephaniah 3:17

15. George MacDonald, quoted in Trevor Hart, *Christian History & Biography*.

16. Chris Martin, quoted in Brian Hiatt, "The Jesus of Uncool," *Rolling Stone*, June 2008.

17. Dorothy Sayers, *The Mind of the Maker* (New York: HarperCollins, 1979), p. 65.

Chapter 11

1. Neil Young, "Hey Hey, My My (Into the Black)," *Rust Never Sleeps*, Reprise Records, 1978.

2. Vincent van Gogh, *The Complete Letters*, 393, II, 348, quoted in Don Postema, *Space for God* (Grand Rapids, Mich.: Faith Alive Christian Resources, 1983, 1997), p. 23.

3. J. R. R. Tolkien, quoted in Joseph Pearce, *Tolkien: Man and Myth* (San Francisco: Ignatius Press, 1998), p. 104.

4. Frederick Buechner, *Telling the Truth: The Gospel as Tragedy, Comedy, & Fairy Tale* (New York: HarperOne, 1977), p. 21.

5. Robert Farrar Capon, *The Parables of Grace* (Grand Rapids, Mich.: Eerdmans, 1988), pp. 3-4.

6. Buechner, *Telling the Truth*, p. 16.

7. Madeleine L'Engle, *Penguins and Golden Calves* (Colorado Springs: Waterbrook Press, 1996), p. 11.

Chapter 12

1. Christopher Alexander, *The Timeless Way of Building* (New York: Oxford University Press, 1979), p. 7.

2. This quote was sent to the author by a church member quoting Gideon Strauss in this online article: http://www.cardus.ca/columns/491/.

3. Alexander, *The Timeless Way of Building*, p. 549.

4. Richard J. Mouw, *When the Kings Come Marching In: Isaiah and the New Jerusalem* (Grand Rapids: Eerdmans, 2002), p. 19.

5. From http://www.ted.com/speakers/eric_sanderson.html.

6. Eric Sanderson, "Eric Sanderson Pictures New York—Before the City," lecture transcript at http://www.ted.com/talks/eric_sanderson_pictures_new_york_before_the_city.html.

READER DISCUSSION GUIDE

1. What do you think is the author's main point? (Back up your answer with quotes and passages from the book.) In your opinion, does the author succeed in communicating this point to the reader?

2. What's the significance of the Metallica story, and why do you think the author begins there?

3. In chapter 2 the author relates some life-changing events from his personal life. How did you react to these events? How did they fit with the book's overall message?

4. The author uses many examples, everything from popular culture, to art, to sports, to fashion. Which example(s) spoke most effectively to you?

5. Beyond the two introductory chapters, did one chapter particularly stick in your mind? Why?

6. If you're reading this book in a group, share with the others a particular section or passage that especially moved or motivated you.

7. How will your life and faith be different after reading this book?